32 Yolks

32 Yolks

From My Mother's Table
to Working the Line

Eric Ripert

with Veronica Chambers

Random House | New York

2017 Random House Trade Paperback Edition

Published in the United States by Random House,
an imprint and division of Penguin Random House LLC, New York.

RANDOM HOUSE and the HOUSE colophon are registered trademarks of
Penguin Random House LLC.

Originally published in hardcover in the United States by Random House,
an imprint and division of Penguin Random House LLC, in 2016.

LIBRARY OF CONGRESS CATALOGING-IN-PUBLICATION DATA
Names: Ripert, Eric. | Chambers, Veronica.
Title: 32 yolks : from my mother's table to working the line / Eric Ripert, with Veronica Chambers.
Other titles: Thirty-two yolks.
Description: New York: Random House, 2016.
Identifiers: LCCN 2015050280 | ISBN 9780812983067 (trade paperback: acid-free paper) |
ISBN 9780679644460 (ebook)
Subjects: LCSH: Ripert, Eric. | Ripert, Eric—Childhood and youth. | Cooks—France—
Paris—Biography. | Restauranteurs—France—Paris—Biography. | Cooking, French. |
Cooking—France—Paris. | Coming of age—France—Paris. | Paris (France)—
Biography. | BISAC: COOKING / Regional & Ethnic / French. |
BIOGRAPHY & AUTOBIOGRAPHY / Personal Memoirs.
Classification: LCC TX649.R57 A3 2016 | DDC 641.5092—dc23
LC record available at http://lccn.loc.gov/2015050280

Printed in the United States of America on acid-free paper

randomhousebooks.com

2 4 6 8 9 7 5 3 1

Book design by Susan Turner

To Adrien and André,
Sandra, and my mother, Monique

32 Yolks

⋮⋮⋮

1

::::

First, Dessert: Chocolate Mousse

Two things happened the year I turned eleven: my father died and I became friends with my first professional chef, a guy named Jacques.

My mother, distressed at my sadness over the loss of my father, tried to cure it with the one thing she knew I still loved: an extraordinary meal. One day, after she closed her shop, she announced that we wouldn't be going home to have dinner with her new husband, Hugo, and my baby sister. Instead we were going to the restaurant in the same complex of shops as her own, Chez Jacques.

"It is almost impossible to get a table," my mother said, smiling conspiratorially. "But why don't you and I go, just the two of us?"

I smiled for the first time in weeks. A night out alone with my mother? At an exclusive restaurant? It was like Christmas had come early.

As we approached Chez Jacques, my mother whispered, "Let me do the talking. They say the chef is a lunatic."

We were greeted at the door by Mercedes Quillacq, a voluptuous blond Spanish woman in her midforties. I had never met her but she greeted my mother as if they were old friends, and she seated us with a flourish that implied we were honored guests. The restaurant was rustic and simple. I would later learn that Jacques had built the entire establishment himself and that the dining room was actually the first floor of the family home. There were maybe twenty seats and an open plan kitchen, which was unusual for the time. There was no menu, just a set meal for the night. You ate what Jacques prepared, and you paid a hefty price for the pleasure.

From my seat at the table I could see Jacques at work in the kitchen: short and muscular, he wore a white chef's jacket with short sleeves and sweated with the force of a man who was all at once chef, sous-chef, and dishwasher. In one pot, he cooked pasta. In another, he made green beans. The industrial oven churned out culinary masterpieces, seemingly on its own. Now there's a platter of caramel pork. Look, there's a *camembert en chemise* (a version of *brie en croute*). And is that a roast duck? Watching Jacques cook for an entire restaurant, alone and happy in his kitchen, was like going to the circus and watching a master juggler spin a hundred plates. I was mesmerized.

I quickly learned that while the food was indeed legendary, part of what kept Chez Jacques packed was the show he put on. You did not choose to eat at Chez Jacques. Jacques chose you.

Ten minutes after we sat down, the door opened. A well-dressed man walked in and greeted Jacques, whose eyes immediately narrowed.

"Get out!" he snarled.

The man was understandably startled and tried to politely introduce himself. "Uh, *je suis Monsieur Veysette. . . .*"

"Who sent you?"

"Uh . . ."

"Get out!" Jacques yelled, and so the man did as he asked and left.

My mother and I sat in silence, watching the drama unfold with both amusement and awe. My pleasure in being there grew, just knowing that we had been lucky to be let in the front door.

A few minutes later, another couple arrived.

"Who sent you?" Jacques barked.

"No one. We saw . . ."

"Welcome, welcome," Jacques said, suddenly switching to the warm tone of a maître'd in a famed Parisian bistro. "Mercedes, please see to it that they get the best table!"

My mother whispered to me, "Chef Jacques is known for kicking even the most elite residents of Andorra out of his restaurant. He takes great pleasure in telling the richest people in town to go screw themselves, but the food is so good, they always come back." She went on to explain that Jacques was ex–French Legion and he wasn't impressed with power. He'd survived the Battle of Dien Bien Phu; he didn't care about the vice-president of the local hydroelectric company or a retired British footballer. Naturally, the spectacle only made Chez Jacques more of a destination. "Whatever you do," my mother warned, "don't ask for salt."

When the dishes arrived, it was clear that we were being presented with more than a meal: this was a gift. The salad was composed as if Jacques had spent the afternoon in the garden, picking each green leaf himself. The *coq au vin* was so rich and satisfying that I had to resist the urge to lick the plate when I was done. When the meal was over, Jacques sent over not two small bowls of chocolate mousse, but nearly a tub of the stuff. My eyes widened at the heft of it; then I quickly and happily polished off the whole dish.

Jacques walked over to the table just as I was shoveling the last heaping spoon of mousse into my mouth. He looked pleased.

"The young man has a good appetite," he said, winking at me.

"*C'est trop, Monsieur Jacques,*" I replied, respectfully. And it was—the very best meal I'd ever had.

"Do you want a tour of the factory?" Jacques asked, gesturing for me to follow him to the kitchen.

My mother nodded her permission and I eagerly followed Jacques back to the kitchen and propped myself onto a barstool for a better view. I pointed at the salads Jacques was making.

"How did you get the vinaigrette so creamy?" I asked.

He smiled at the question. "That's a secret," he said. "Come back one day and I'll show you."

The next day after school, instead of heading to the stockroom above my mother's boutique, I went to Chez Jacques. I sat on the same barstool, eating bowl after bowl of *baba au rhum,* and listened as he told me stories about his years in the military.

Jacques was what was called a *titi Parisien,* a kind of

scrappy, working-class guy who grew up on the not-fancy streets of Paris, like Robert De Niro in New York. He spent his career as a parachutist with the French army and had done tours of duty in Vietnam, Egypt, and Algeria. I learned more about history from him than I did from any schoolbook.

"You've read about the coalition between Germany, France, and Great Britain against Egypt when they tried to nationalize the Suez Canal?" he asked as he rubbed a leg of lamb with salt for that evening's meal.

I had never heard of the Suez Canal, but I nodded my head vigorously in the hopes that he'd keep talking and serving me sweets.

"*Alors.* Each country had their own black market of goods," Jacques explained. "Crates of everything from caviar to licorice. Well, one day, we heard that the British had gotten ahold of some fresh vegetables, so we traded with them—a crate of whiskey for a crate of arugula, endives, and romaine. They just wanted to get drunk! But we said, 'The French must eat the way God intended man to eat!'"

He laughed so hard at the memory that he had to brace himself on the counter. "Can you imagine? Trading whiskey for some greens? But that is war, young man. That is what war is really about: going after the thing you didn't value until you were in the position to lose it."

I was only a kid but I thought I understood what he meant, because I had, that afternoon, spent one of the happiest days in recent memory. The school year loomed ahead, and I was sure that nothing would top the few hours I had spent watching Jacques cook and listening to his stories about parachuting out of planes and conducting secret maneuvers in foreign lands.

My mother worked six days a week at her boutique, but
she cooked like a Michelin-starred chef every single night.
The table was always set with fresh flowers and a beautiful
tablecloth. She shopped every day at the markets. We began
each meal with a delicious starter: maybe an onion soup or a
big rustic salad made of blanched and raw vegetables, apple,
avocado, radishes, potato, *haricots verts,* corn—all from a
roadside market, not the grocery store. For the main course,
there would be something cooked *à la minute,* like a pepper
steak, or something she'd prepped since the morning, like a
roast shoulder of lamb. There was always dessert too: a fruit
dish, like pears in red wine, on the weekdays and something
more elaborate, like a flan or a mixed berry tart, on her day
off. It was a badge of honor for my mother that at a time when
women were asking if they could have it all, she did.

That evening when she came to collect me, her eyes went
straight to the dirty dessert bowl sitting next to me. She knew
me well enough to know that there was no way I had eaten just
one serving. I could tell she was annoyed at what was certain
to be an enormous bill and at my rudeness in ruining my appetite for the dinner she'd prepared at home.

But when my mother asked Jacques for the bill, throwing
me an impatient glare, he just waved her off.

"No charge, madame," he said. "The boy has been washing dishes all day. It is I who should pay him." Then he winked
at me and smiled.

This was, needless to say, a lie for my protection, and the
pure tenderness of the gesture almost made me cry.

"Come back anytime," Jacques said. I wondered if he
meant it or if he was just being polite.

"Tomorrow?" I asked, shyly.

"Why not?" he answered.

"Will there be chocolate mousse the next time?" I asked, feeling bolder.

Jacques laughed, a full-bodied laugh that I would get to know well. And my mother, who in those days did not laugh very often, laughed too.

"There is always chocolate mousse at Chez Jacques," he said.

Proust had his madeleine and because of Jacques, I have my mousse. Every time I dig into a bowl of that chocolate velvet, I am a kid again, running to Chez Jacques after school. It is the taste of friendship. It is the taste of belly laughs, and war stories, and the memory of a man who could jump out of planes and make a leg of lamb with equal amounts of skill and ardor. But more than anything, chocolate mousse is the taste of being welcomed; of Chez Jacques, where for me, the door was always open.

2

My Father's Castle

In 1961, Paul Newman and Sidney Poitier came to Paris to make a movie about jazz, love, and possibility. In the film, Paul Newman plays a jazz musician who sees the most beautiful girl, played by Diahann Carroll, while walking down the street. She's not interested in him, but she takes a liking to his friend, Sidney Poitier, and it just so happens that her pal, Joanne Woodward, thinks Paul Newman is kind of cute. So the pairs switch around and go about the business of falling in love, but in the end, each of the men and each of the women must go off on their own path. There is no happily ever after for these couples, only happy to have met you.

Not too long after that movie debuted, my parents met in

the south of France. In time, they would do their own switching around of partners and falling in and out of love. But where the lovers in *Paris Blues* had only themselves to worry about, my parents' choices affected me too, and I felt shuffled and tossed about by all of the changes. Despite all that would come afterward, the first five years of my life were so happy and bright that decades cannot diminish the sunshine and warmth that I feel when I look back at that time. My parents' greatest gift to me was this: a model of love that was so big, it felt like the stuff of movies and songs. It wasn't an endless love, but it was a gift all the same.

This is where it began: on a road lined with olive trees, on a bright summer day in Cagnes-sur-Mer, the largest suburb of the city of Nice. My mother, Monique, was waiting for the No. 44 bus. She had golden brown skin, the skin of a girl who has spent her whole life in sunny places—Morocco and the south of France. She was tall and thin, with hair as black as a raven that hit her back at an alluring spot. Her eyes were rimmed with kohl; her lips were a deep ruby red. My mother was just an eighteen-year-old shopgirl, but she had mastered the look of the jet set. She carried herself with confidence—even a slight arrogance—that men found irresistible. She was a prize, and she knew it.

My father, André, was ten years her senior. He was handsome and he knew it, the golden boy and oldest son of a farming family in Nîmes. He was born at the dawn of the Second World War. Like many in France, his family suffered greatly through the wars and he was determined to make a success of himself. He never wanted to feel hunger or deprivation again.

My father saw my mother standing by the bus stop wearing a miniskirt that showed off her long legs, and he was taken with her immediately. He was driving in his most prized possession, a red Peugeot convertible.

"Hello, beautiful," he said. "Where are you off to?"

My mother explained that she was going into town to meet a friend, to see a movie.

My father dismissed this suggestion out of hand. "You are going to sit in a dark room with a group of strangers on this gorgeous day? That's madness."

"What else do you have in mind?" my mother asked.

"Let's stroll the coast together," he said.

She gladly canceled her plans and he took her to Monaco.

My father was charming. My mother was daring. And that's how it all began.

My father was the pride of his family. He had worked his way through the ranks of the Banque Nationale de Paris, and had done so well that he was named president of the Cagnes-sur-Mer branch before his thirtieth birthday. He was married once, in his early twenties, to a girl from back home, but the marriage ended before they had children. He was single and well-off on the French Riviera, and my father enjoyed playing the role of a bad boy.

He took my mother to all of the most fabulous parties. The people they rubbed elbows with are like a who's who of France in the 1960s: Over there is the actor Alain Delon, famed for his recent turn as Ripley in *Purple Noon,* the French movie adaptation of the Patricia Highsmith novel *The Talented Mr. Ripley.* Here comes Brigitte Bardot, all blond hair and bosoms, talking animatedly about animal rights. Mingling with them are high-ranking government officials who have traveled to the south to take part in the fun and sun.

Françoise Sagan, the young novelist whose *Bonjour Tristesse* had been an international bestseller, was a frequent visitor to St. Tropez during those years. My parents would see her at parties. She grew up not far away in the region of Carjac, in the southwest of France. She was not much older than my mother, and she represented a new generation of women that my mother would be a part of, women who were lauded for their brains as well as their beauty.

On Sundays, my parents picnicked at the beach, and my father quickly discovered that my mother was a wonderful cook. It was not so much that she was domestically inclined (she had already informed him that she intended to continue to work after marriage and that she never wanted to be financially dependent on a man), but for my mother, cooking well was a matter of aesthetics, what she saw as an indication of good breeding and taste. She was the type of person who wanted everything to be just so, so she practiced and read books about cooking and perfected each recipe until she was proud.

A few months after their first meeting, my father proposed, and two years after they were married, I was born. My parents moved into a little house in St. Tropez. It was a stucco house with a garden out back and for a while, a different fairy tale took root. My father continued to succeed at work. As soon as I was old enough for daycare, my mother got a job at a boutique in St. Tropez. Although she was only in her early twenties, she was capable and by the time I was two years old, she was named *directrice,* manager of the store. They were happy with their careers and happy with each other, and for the first few years of my life, all was well.

. . .

My father was a peculiar mixture of traits. On the one hand, he was politically conservative, as one might expect of someone who had built his career in finance. When it came to his work, he was disciplined, focused, and unwavering. But at home, he was a different man. His whole life away from the bank was the opposite of everything the business world represented. At work, he was serious, traditional in dress and demeanor. At home, it was the future and the fringes that most interested him. He loved the circus. He loved technology, especially photography, and he was always taking pictures when I was a baby. By the time I was a toddler, he had upgraded from a simple Leica to an early version of a Super 8 motion picture camera. He loved sports, and every Saturday morning, we took off for the great outdoors. In the summer, it was the beach, where he taught me how to swim and snorkel and fish. In the winter, he hiked, climbing snowy mountains with athletic determination.

My father had a set routine in the morning: shower, shave, dress (he favored a dark suit and a light shirt, conservative but still sharp), eat breakfast, brush teeth, slap on aftershave, kiss son (that would be me), and go. As a chef, my brain holds a catalogue of scents, and the first, most powerful one is this: my father's aftershave, accompanied by the cool tingle and slight damp of his cheek as he wrapped me in his arms and kissed me goodbye before he left for work.

In the evening, when he returned, my father would change out of his suit into a plain T-shirt, shorts, and flip-flops and go out back to work in his garden. Tending to the garden was one of his greatest pleasures. It was a way of transforming the stress of the day into something alive and growing. He often said, "I am proud to be a *paysan*," using the term for a simple country farmer, like his ancestors.

Though my mother's cooking ruled my childhood, my earliest food memories are not of eating her food. When I was very small, I ate from my father's garden: tomatoes and fennel in the late summer, steamed potato and eggplant in the fall, snap peas sautéed in butter and salt in the spring.

But the dish I remember most of all was not from any garden. Having read an article that said you can exponentially increase children's intelligence by feeding them brains, my mother tried night after night to get me to eat fricasseed lamb brains. And night after night, I perfected the art of throwing the brains across the room, using my teaspoon as a catapult.

My father had many interests, but none was as great as his passion for jazz. Nearly a million African Americans served in World War II, and jazz was the music they brought with them. While jazz had been popular as early as the 1920s, it was really in this period that the form of the music—innovative, revolutionary, a pastiche of history and culture—reflected the cultural moment so powerfully. All throughout Europe, jazz was the music of the Resistance and it symbolized hope, freedom, and a joy that felt precious and fleeting. As the German pianist Jutta Hipp once explained, "Americans won't be able to understand this, but to us, jazz is some kind of religion. We really had to fight for it and I remember nights when we didn't go down to the bomb shelter because we listened to [jazz] records. We just had the feeling that they were not our enemies and even though the bombs crashed around us . . . we felt safe."

My father came from a musical family. His father, Antonin, was just sixteen when he was called to serve in World War I. He rode a horse and played the trumpet for the cavalry,

blasting out the short melodies that were the military's signals
to their soldiers. The bugle calls were loud and soldiers relied
on them to carry messages above the noise and confusion of
the battlefield.

Antonin survived the war and married my grandmother
Emilienne, who played the violin. They both loved music,
opera especially, and it was a love that sustained them through
some of France's toughest times. Antonin and Emilienne had
five children, including my father, when World War II broke
out and Antonin was called to play the trumpet for the army
again.

France was very poor and the south of France was poorer
still. When my grandfather returned to his home in Carpen-
tras after the war, he found that he couldn't make a living from
his farm anymore, so he moved the family to Nîmes, where he
found a job as an accountant for a mining company. My father
was the only child to pick up an instrument. He chose to play
trumpet, just as his father did. My father went to university
and all throughout his college years continued to study music
at the conservatory.

In France at this time, a year of military service was mandatory. My father took his trumpet with him into service and it
was there, as a soldier, that he fell in love with jazz. The music,
which he heard on the radio and in the dance halls that the
soldiers frequented on their furloughs, became the soundtrack
to my parents' short, passionate marriage.

My mother loved to throw parties and my father was a
natural-born entertainer, so they threw lots and lots of parties.
When we were happy, our house was filled with music—Chet
Baker on the turntable or my father, trumpet in hand, capti-
vating a small crowd of friends with the words and rhythms of

Louis Armstrong. We were a young French family—Maman, Papa, and myself—and our home was a salon. By the time I was four years old, our home had become the center of their social circle. There were parties every weekend and these are some of my earliest memories: happy people, my mother cooking, my father playing the trumpet, rooms that smelled of drink and smoke, long nights filled with music and laughter. Every night, just before the parties started to ramp up, my parents would slip away from the festivities to put me to bed. Mine was just a plain wooden cot, but I liked to pretend it was a rocket ship.

Later, when things were bad, and later still, when bad went to worse, food became my main source of comfort, my most consistent pleasure. But in the beginning, when I was too small to read or write, when I didn't know left from right or how to tie my own shoes, there was this: my mother, beaming at me with her eyes, bright and starry, and my father serenading me to sleep with Louis Armstrong on his horn.

3

:::

My Mother's Kitchen

I don't know when my father began to stray, but once he did, the affairs were frequent and egregious. My mother is always careful to tell me that she was "no angel either"—she too liked to flirt, and perhaps she took it even further with an affair or two of her own. But my father's assignations broke her down. "It's not that cheating changes the other person," she has explained to me. "Your father was still very much the same man he always was: smart, handsome, funny. It's how it changed *me* that I could not take."

I think I understand what she means, because I remember the shift. My mother, who was once all hugs and smiles, became pinched and closed off. Always a woman who liked to sing around the house, she replaced songs with screams and shouts. I rarely saw her in tears, but she always looked as if she'd just been crying. Her eyes would be red, her mascara would run, and the cat eyes she drew on with liner to elongate the almond shape of her eyes would look shaky, as if she'd drawn them with trembling hands. It was scary, the way I learned how people could change. I look back at it now and I want to say, "It was nothing. Relationships fall apart. Life is complicated. People get divorced." But it wasn't nothing. It wasn't nothing then, it isn't nothing now. I can still remember the terror of not being able to breathe as they argued, the way my lungs would contract as if a monster was sitting on my chest and wouldn't move: all of those nights when I was supposed to be sleeping, but I couldn't close my eyes for fear that the world as I knew it would end before I could open them again.

During this time, my father got a promotion and we moved from St. Tropez to a town on the coast called Les Sables d'Olonne. I have few happy memories of that place. The night that I understood, without a doubt, that my parents' marriage was ending, I was in my room, pretending to be asleep. My mother's voice rose to a scream while my father's stayed low, trying to keep her from losing control. It didn't work.

"*Combien de temps . . . ?*" she shouted. "I knew . . . how *dare* you . . ." There was an edge to her voice, one I could only compare to the sound the dog down the street made when I poked a stick between the slats of the fence. And then the china began to crash. Terrified, I cracked open my door and peeked into the dining room.

My parents argued a lot, but this was different. It felt as though all of the bad feelings between them had finally exploded and everything was burning to the ground. There was no going back. My mother was unloading their wedding china from the vitrine and throwing it at the wall behind my father as he stood there, helpless. Even at five, I knew how proud my mother was of her porcelain. It was shocking to watch it come to such a violent end.

By now, I was standing in the hall. My father had seen me leaning against the wall in my pajamas and pleaded with my mother, whose back was to me: "Stop! You'll traumatize Eric!" he yelled. My mother launched a tureen at his head and then crumpled into tears.

My father guided me back into my room and tucked me in, holding me as I cried in confusion. "It's going to be fine," he repeated as he smoothed my hair. "Sometimes your mother gets upset." It felt like hours until I fell asleep.

The next morning, my father woke me up for breakfast.

"It's just the two of us," he said. "Your mother's not feeling well."

When I said that she seemed more angry than sick, he pinched my cheek and told me that one day I would learn more than I might ever want to know about women and their bad tempers.

He didn't mention what had happened the night before. Instead, he apologized for a few days before when he'd read me a book about a famous bullfighter. This was something upsetting that he could actually discuss. Growing up in Nîmes, a southern city with deep Roman and Spanish influences, my father had gone to bullfights in the ancient arena. He always talked about the day we'd see our first bullfight there. But a few pages into the book, I told him I would never go. Inside were pictures of men on horses lancing bulls with beribboned spears while the bulls gored the horses' sides,

and then pictures of the bulls' corpses being dragged cere-
moniously through the dust, trailing blood. The image was
meant to be triumphant, but when I saw it, I started to cry.
How could they be so unfair? How could you treat an animal
with such cruelty?

My dad told me he couldn't imagine how such a mischievous kid could be so sensitive to other people's pain. "Next
time you torture your babysitter to the point that she doesn't
want to come back, I want you to remember what you're saying," he said, laughing.

He set our dishes in the sink, put on his suit jacket and tie,
and left for the bank. I stood on the balcony and watched him
get in his car. After he drove away, my mother came out and
asked what I was doing.

It was summer, so I didn't have to go to school. Instead, I
spent the day watching from the hallway as my mother silently
packed a suitcase.

We didn't leave that night. Or the next. Instead, my parents performed fake-happy conversations at the dinner table
for weeks on end. As sweet as they tried to be with me, I could
still feel the seriousness and tension weighing down every
word. I could see the pain in their eyes and hear the strain in
their voices. During those meals, a heavy sadness filled the
house, quiet and intense. My family was broken. So, when
they called me into the living room and sat me down on the
green velvet sofa, I was prepared.

My father fidgeted with a crystal paperweight on the Chi-
nese coffee table, whose carved legs served as an off-road
track for my model cars. "Your mother and I are going to try
living apart for a while," he said.

I asked them what "a while" meant and they both laughed.

"It'll be good for you because you'll be able to travel," my mother said. She was wearing the smile she used when telling me that the doctor's needle was going to help me, so I should just relax. "You can spend time with me and with your father. . . ."

"Until perhaps we get back together," he said, looking at my mother hopefully.

"Yes," she chimed in. "Until then. Perhaps. *D'accord?*"

My mother began to cry. Then my father too. This was the worst sign yet. I joined them.

Perhaps if they hadn't been so happy to begin with, the end would have been less heartbreaking. But it was like a part of each of us died in that apartment the day my mother and I moved out. My father, who was an expert at putting on a sunny appearance, did the best job of seeming unchanged. But in the years that followed my parents' divorce, I would come to see his loss, his grief. For my mother and I, the pain was more immediate and easier to see. My mother, who was so beautiful, became like a model who has smiled so many times, her smile is frozen, patently fake. Even when she seemed to be in a good mood, she showed a studied grin that did not match the faraway look in her eyes. As for me, I went from being a happy kid to a kind of pint-sized depressive. From the time I was five until I went away to cooking school and for many years after, I was rarely truly happy—just different degrees of sad.

It was late afternoon when my father drove my mother and me to our new home in St. Tropez, an investment property he owned there. He was dressed in his weekend casual: a polo shirt, a pair of khakis, leather loafers. It was as if we were all on our way to a country getaway, the way my father made cheerful conversation the whole drive. He rolled down the window and breathed in deeply. "Can you smell it?" he said. "The orange trees, the lemon trees? Look over there, a vineyard. Oh, it's Bandol. Provence makes the best rosé in the world, that's why the Provençal are so happy."

Every time my father turned around to talk to me on the drive to St. Tropez, which was often, he would take his eyes off the road and my mother would flinch, sucking in a gust of breath as if she half-expected the car to swerve at any moment and wrap around a tree.

He told me that he would write to me often and that he wanted me to write back—even if it was just a picture on a postcard. It was 1971, and no one used the phone to keep in touch. Phone calls were for short local conversations. My parents called each other on the aqua and white rotary phone to confirm meeting times and to give each other brief reminders, their sentences quick and precise.

In all the years of their marriage and all the years after, I was never summoned to the phone to speak to my mother or father, wasn't prompted to pick up the receiver and tell my grandmother that I loved her or tell my grandfather that I missed him, even though I did. My parents never called their parents on the phone unless there was an emergency. It was too expensive and even though they were young and successful, they came from modest means and they had modest ways.

My father swung around, one hand on the wheel, and tried to catch my eyes. He wanted me to know that he meant business. "Let me hear from you, Eric," he told me. "We must stay close. You are my only son, the last Ripert." Then he grinned. "I am the great Ripert, but you are the last. Just because we are not eating breakfast together and having dinner together all the time, it does not change anything. We must not let this distance become a wedge between us. We will write letters and when you come on vacation, we will have grand adventures, like Zorro."

I perked up at this: no one was better than my father at playing games of pretend.

When we arrived at the apartment building, I looked around, confused.

"Where is the house?" I asked.

"It is not a house," my mother said. "It's an apartment. You'll like it. The school is just down the street and the building is full of kids. Come, Eric, let's look."

She gave me her tight new smile, and I could tell that she was trying to sell the place to me, which was surprising. In France, parents do not cater to children. You can walk through a playground, a department store, or any bakery and you will hear a hundred times, *"C'est moi qui décide."* It is me who decides. French parents expect a sense of hierarchy and a respect from their children. You give them the answers and they accept them. But as we stood outside our new home, I could feel my mother softening, and because it was so uncharacteristic and her eyes were so sad, it seemed like she was not only giving in, but giving up.

My father leaned in to kiss her on both cheeks and she stiffened in his embrace. Then he bent down to embrace me. Grabbing me into his arms, he lifted me as if I were a plane and he spun me around in the air.

I jutted my arms forward and straightened my legs and announced, "I'm Batman!"

"Very good!" my father said. "Are you flying?"

"Yes," I said, as he moved me through the air. "I'm flying!"

When he put me down, I could see in his eyes, in the curve of his shoulders, and in the downturn of his lips that he was tired too. "Keep flying, Eric," he said, but his words felt hollow and halfhearted. Then he walked back to the car and as he put his key in the door, a puzzled look crossed his face, as if he were an amnesiac who wasn't sure where he had put his wife and son, as if he were a man who had misplaced his whole life.

At the door of the apartment building, two men stood smoking cigarettes, and they looked at my mother hungrily. She cut the ogling off with a single devastating "don't even think about it" glare.

I couldn't tell what she was thinking as she climbed the stairs to our new second-floor flat. She seemed at sea, like one of those teenage girls in a French New Wave movie. They were beautiful, these girls, and I liked to look at their pictures on the big posters outside of the cinema in town. But they also looked spacey and unsure, as if they themselves had no idea how the movie might end.

My mother had always looked older than her age, but on this night, she looked very young. Instead of her usual impeccably coiffed waves, her hair was pulled back into a simple ponytail, and her face was scrubbed free of makeup.

Apparently, I wasn't the only one who thought my mother looked like a teenager, because as she stood at the landing of the second floor, the door to a nearby apartment flew open and a woman called out, "Giselle, I hear you on the steps! I told you, no going out on a school night!"

When my mother turned to look at her, the woman said,

"Excuse me, I'm sorry, mademoiselle." Then, upon seeing me, "I mean, madame." The woman had changed her tone, not wanting to insult my mom by suggesting that she was an unwed mother.

But it was exactly onto this precipice that my mother had fallen. Too young to be a madame, but too much the divorcée to be a mademoiselle. She had been the first of her friends to be married and now was the first to get divorced. She was twenty-six years old.

We spent just a few months in that studio apartment in St. Tropez. Then my mother got the opportunity to open her own boutique, so we moved to a small town called Revel. We moved into the guesthouse of a farm, which I liked much better than the noisy apartment building, and because she was new in town, there was no babysitter. My mother kept me close under her wing. We came home for dinner and to sleep, but we spent our afternoons and weekends at my mother's boutique.

My mother, who had a discerning eye for fashion and a knack for putting even affordable clothes together, was quickly a success in Revel as the local women clamored to see what she brought back from her shopping trips to Paris. It was, I think, some small consolation to my mother. Her marriage may have failed, but she had not failed at her goal of financial independence. My mother took me with her on trips to Paris, and she made sure that I was well dressed and well groomed when I went to visit my father every five or six weeks. Even at that age, I knew how I appeared—the only child of two well-off parents, shuttled back and forth in first-class train cars, eating meals at Michelin-starred restaurants. I was, my cousins joked, a little prince. But in the novel by Antoine de Saint-Exupéry, the little prince is not notable because he has noble blood. The entire throughline of the story is that he is lonely, and inhabits a "mysterious place, the land of tears."

When I began first grade in Revel, I made a game of getting through the entire school day without saying a word. I shrugged when the teachers asked me questions, shook my head "no" when the other kids invited me to play at recess. After school, I stayed in the back of my mother's boutique until she could drive us home to the little farmhouse. It was there that I released the energy that had been pent up all day. I bounced off the walls of the storeroom while I was supposed to be doing my homework and refused to write letters to my father like I was repeatedly asked.

My mother had a hard time getting me to talk to or be affectionate with her. I blamed her for my parents' breakup. It was she, after all, who had broken the wedding china, and who did all the yelling and screaming. When I was feeling mean, I would ask her, "Why did you send my father away?" and watch as tears welled up. She would look at me as if I'd punched her, and the pained look on her face gave me a kind of satisfaction. I studied her grimaces the same way I looked on as insects squirmed when I took them apart, wing by wing.

After my parents' divorce, the only time I felt close to my mother was in the kitchen. From the second she put on her apron, I followed her every move. My anger disappeared and I was finally able to calm down and focus as I watched her in that tiny room, making meals that I could tell were intended to make me happy. I was so entranced that I'd even answer her questions about what I'd done in school. I listened closely as she told me stories about her childhood in Morocco, how she learned to cook French dishes from her mother, and the cookbooks by great chefs that she bought as soon as she started earning her own money. My mother was never more expressive of her love than when she was in the kitchen. She was reserved by nature, and while she hugged and kissed me plenty, she was never one to smother me with physical affection. But she made it clear that everything she prepared in the kitchen was done with the hopes of pleasing me. She reminded me that I'd always loved to eat: "When you were a baby," she'd tell me, "you drank so much formula that we had to go to the doctor to make sure you were normal. Even he was surprised!" Sitting on my chair in that tiny farm kitchen felt intimate and special. That room was sacred.

Although I wasn't allowed to help with the meal proper, my mother gave me little things to do. She let me flick on the light of the oven to see how her cake was rising. She gave me balls of dough to shape into deformed loaves of "bread." I was fascinated by the act of cooking—how sugar, butter, apples, and dough magically transformed into a richly burnished *tarte tatin*. (Flipping it from hot skillet to plate was another favorite magic trick.) I loved the craftsmanship—how my mother artfully folded thin pieces of rice paper around ground pork, crab, and vegetables to create delicate, transparent spring rolls, which the French called *nem*. When I'd ask why she put them in a cold sauté pan filled with oil before turning on the heat, she'd explain that it made them crisper and fully cooked inside. Later, as my teeth shattered the golden rice-paper wrapper, I'd ask her to explain it again so I could make them myself one day. I loved the constant motion of cooking the way some kids loved sports. She spent hours assembling her couscous, starting with the mise en place. Next, she began her lamb tagine, flavored with the peel of lemons that she buried in a jar of salt until they became moist and candy-like. While the tagine simmered in its cone-topped earthen pot, she rolled damp semolina between her palms until fine, fluffy blond grains of couscous showered into the bowl, ready to be steamed. I was fixated on whatever it was her hands were doing as she spoke, the slow, intricate dance that always ended deliciously. It was an incredible show.

In the dining room, she taught me to set the table with ironed napkins and good china and silver, even for just the two of us. It didn't occur to me until I began working in restaurants myself years later that she was educating me in what she called *l'art de la table*, teaching me the importance of elegant presentation because she believed that it made the food taste even better. To her, the entire meal was a creative act, an expression of refinement and taste. There were always flowers, candles, and a starched tablecloth, whether we were eating crab soufflé or *onglet* and *frites*. We even changed plates between courses like they did in restaurants. I grew up thinking that everyone ate this way.

Besides spoiling me at the table, my mother also indulged my appetite at the supermarket. I'd tell her exactly which *jambon de Paris* and yogurt I wanted from the shelves. I was extremely picky about my favorite variety of Petit Suisse cheese, not to mention the brand of mini-toasts that I had for breakfast, along with the butter and jam. She usually rushed me past the cookie aisle, but I didn't mind; there was always something better to eat at home. For me, watching her make pastry was pure magic—and then, of course, there was the pastry itself. But once the dishes had been washed and the *tarte tatin* put away for tomorrow's snack, my anger at my mother and my hunger for my father returned.

4

:::

Then There Was Hugo

After a reasonable mourning period, my mother began to date, and it wasn't long before it seemed like she was dating all the time. The babysitters who now sometimes watched me after school until my mother closed the shop were staying long after I'd gone to bed.

The men my mother dated took no interest in me, nor I in them. One guy was always slurring and stumbling, a glass in his hand. Another I saw from my spying station upstairs; he cornered my mom in the hallway and grabbed her by the neck until she screamed and wrestled herself free and kicked him out of our apartment. And while I would have liked to spend more time with the famous rugby player she dated for a few months, the truth is that I didn't mind being sent to stay with my grandfather and grandmother—his second wife, Maguy— for long weekends and short vacations.

On the rare days my mom didn't have a date, I would head to the boutique after school and wait, bored out of my mind, until she could drive us home. One day when I arrived at my mother's boutique, there was a man at the counter, showing her pictures of clothes in a big binder.

"Eric, this is Hugo," she said, patting her hair. "He's a distributor for a sportswear company."

Hugo shook my hand, even though I was only six. He looked like Charles Bronson, pre-mustache.

"Your mother says you're a real gourmand," he said.

"That's because she's the best cook in Revel!"

Hugo was there after school another time, and then another, usually with something for me from the bakery in his town. He definitely came across as a bad boy, and with his pomaded hair and louche demeanor, the Charles Bronson resemblance didn't seem like a coincidence. He talked admiringly about gangster movies and I could tell that he tried to cultivate the air of a tough guy.

He invited us out one Sunday for a picnic in the countryside and picked us up in his Mercedes. I had been expecting sandwiches, but he unpacked a tablecloth and set it with real plates, glasses, and silverware. My mother was impressed, and I was happy that she was happy. Over roast pork loin, he explained socialism to me in a way that made sense. I told him how I used to argue with my teachers about the Vietnam War, and Hugo told me that the Vietnamese were fighting for communism, which was kind of like socialism, so it sounded good to me.

After we were finished with lunch, Hugo patiently tried to teach me to fish using leftover baguette. He wasn't my dad—no one, to my mind, was as cool as my dad. But at least he was making an effort.

When he dropped us off, he asked if he could take us mushroom hunting the next weekend. I could see from my mother's expression that she wanted not just a boyfriend, but someone who would be a kind of father figure to me. I silently vowed to give Hugo a chance.

The mushroom hunt was followed by a quail hunt. I was excited to be out in the forest, but I was still just a kid. I didn't know how to follow Hugo silently and he yelled at me for making noise, scaring the birds away. It doesn't take long for a child to figure out how quickly the switch in an adult can flip. When you are small and nothing in the world is truly your choice, you learn to read the adults around you so that you can get what you want: their praise, their affection, their love. I began to see that with Hugo there was very little room for error on my part.

We all shared a love of fine food, and Hugo took my mother and me to the best restaurants in the region. By the time I was in first grade, I was already fond of cheese soufflé, *filet en croute, foie gras, sole meunière,* and stinky cheeses. By the end of the year, the three of us were living in an apartment above the store. My mother was happy for the first time in years, but my impression of Hugo had dimmed.

On Sunday, her one day off, my mom would stay in the bedroom with Hugo until lunchtime, at which point he would come out, knot his foulard, and march me in the direction of the local movie theater, about a mile away. It didn't matter if what was playing was appropriate for children; I was dropped at the curb and left to see Hugo-approved films like *The God-*

father and *The Good, the Bad, and the Ugly,* which give me nightmares to this day.

My mother's business began to boom, which was fortunate because it turned out that Hugo was not the high roller he pretended to be. I could sense my mother's disappointment. She'd married a successful man, but he was unfaithful. She now had a faithful man, but he wasn't successful. She poured her energy into being successful enough for the both of them. Soon, she was able to open a second boutique in the nearby town of Castelnaudary, where I started at a new school.

I had grown jealous of Hugo, and I could tell he was jealous of me too. Now that he'd gotten what he wanted, a different side of him began to emerge. When we went hunting, he'd yell at me in front of my mother, telling me that my clumsiness was scaring away the animals. He'd say I'd never be a good fisherman, or that I was so dumb I couldn't find a wild mushroom if it was glued to my nose.

One weekend, we went into the mountains to go skiing. It was my first time on skis and I kept falling in the snow. Hugo would stand over me, laughing and saying, "You fall so often. Learning how to get up will be your most important skill." Each time, my mother, laughing along with him, reached out with her pole and helped me to my feet. But I began to wonder, what happens when my mother isn't there to pick me up?

When she praised my schoolwork, he criticized it. When she told me I was handsome, he'd say, "Maybe, but you should close your mouth. You look like a mongoloid." (His nickname for me was *gagotte*, which is a horrible French slur used to describe the mentally disabled.)

The only time Hugo and I were civil was at the dinner table.

Please pass the bread.

Yes, thank you!

This blanquette de veau *is perfect, Monique.*

It was a temporary truce, my mother's ironed linen napkins our white flag.

In St. Tropez, before my parents' divorce, my father had worked as the head of the bank in town. The town was crazy in the summer, rife with tourists and yachts full of partying celebrities, but in the winter, it felt more like a small village, where the residents could really mingle and get to know each other. Marcel Pagnol was a customer at my father's bank; over the years the two became quite friendly, and the friendship meant a great deal to my father. Pagnol was a legend in his own time: a novelist, a playwright, and a filmmaker, he was like John Updike, Tennessee Williams, and Woody Allen all rolled into one. He was the first French filmmaker to be elected to L'Académie Française. Founded in 1653 by the chief minister to King Louis XIII, L'Académie consists of just forty members who are known as *immortels:* the immortals. These forty men (back then, they were all men) rule on all matters of the French language, and it is their grave responsibility to guide and shape the evolution of the written and spoken word. Marcel Pagnol's membership in this academy was the equivalent of being knighted by the queen of England.

Pagnol quite liked my father, and he gifted him with an autographed copy of his most famous book, *La Gloire de Mon Père,* or *The Glory of My Father.* Although Pagnol was revered across the country as a cultural genius, in the south where he was born and eventually retired, he was known as the hero of

the *paysan,* the working man. This was especially meaningful
to my father, who prided himself on his humble background.
My father cherished his autographed book and he would show
it off to anyone who came over. Sometimes he took it to work
to show it off to a client.

After the divorce, when my mother packed up our things,
she got her revenge. She hid the book in a box and took it to
our new home. The night my father realized the book was
missing, I witnessed a rare display of fury from him. I could
hear him screaming at my mother through the phone, but she
refused to return it.

The Pagnol book was a trophy and my mother displayed it
on the bookshelf with her favorite novels. Sometimes, I took it
to school to show my teachers. Just having it in my backpack
gave me a kind of courage.

At night was when I missed my father the most. I missed
our ritual of stories and the tenderness of him tucking me in.
On those nights when the ache of not having him in the house
was the worst, I tucked the Pagnol book under my pillow, just
to have some part of him next to me.

After a few months of living with Hugo, I began to feel like
my mother had chosen her boyfriend over me and that she,
like him, was merely tolerating my presence. To get back at
her, the next time I went to see my dad, I took the Marcel
Pagnol book from its place of honor and hid it in my suitcase.

I was so proud to have returned the beloved object to my
father, who was happy I'd thought of him. (He must have
known I'd stolen it from my mother, but he didn't let on.) But
about a week into my visit, my mother called. She and my father got into a vicious argument about the book, with her using
all of her diplomatic resources to get it back. Finally, she told

him that if I didn't bring the book with me, I wouldn't be allowed home.

As I was packing for the drive back, my father handed me the Pagnol.

"I love this book, but apparently so does your mother; please take it back to her," he said.

I nodded, ashamed and embarrassed that my gift had been returned.

My father held me close. "It was lovely to see it again. Thank you, Eric. I'm counting on you to look after it for me."

I nodded and said that I would.

My father drove me to my mother's boutique and told me to wait in the car while he went in for what he knew would be a tongue lashing. After he left, it was my turn.

"I'm glad you've learned how to steal, Eric," my mother said when I got in. "I'm only going to warn you once: if you do that again, you won't live with me anymore. I must be able to trust you."

It was a funny word, *trust*. I loved my parents. With all of their shortcomings, I loved them both mightily. But if you asked me whom I trusted, I could not tell you. I wasn't sure I knew what that word meant.

It was not long before things began to sour between my mother and Hugo. He liked the flash life, but he didn't have the means to take care of my mother the way he did when they were first dating. That money—begged, borrowed, or stolen—was gone. Hugo's job disappeared too, so my mother took him on at her boutique. From their evening arguments, I could tell that Hugo wasn't the help to my mother's business that she hoped he might be.

At night, after she kissed me good night, my mother was careful to put on the record player, but I could still hear their heated conversations:

"Hugo, you are supposed to sell the clothes, not yourself."

"I am only flirting to flatter, my dearest," Hugo cooed. "Flattery encourages the customers to buy." It was his attempt at being seductive, and even just listening to him be so smarmy made me want to throw up.

My mother, I know, was sipping from a cup of tea. She had made herself a pot of *verveine* (lemon verbena) to calm her nerves; I could smell it steeping.

"Flatter the clothes, not the women," my mother sighed. "You say, 'Wow, you look beautiful in that dress,' or 'That is the height of sophistication, what's the occasion?'"

My mother had already left one man for cheating. She did not want to leave another. But more important, she had built her business herself, from the ground up. She was strong enough to deal with Hugo's flirting if it was harmless, but she would not abide his lack of work and how it was hurting our family income.

Their relationship shifted, and my mother no longer sent me to the movies on Sunday afternoon. She did not seem to have any interest in spending time alone with Hugo at all. So when she was not around, which was roughly Monday through Friday, from 3 P.M. until 8:30 or 9 P.M. and all day on Saturday— the boutique's busiest day—Hugo and I were left alone.

It was a war, and there were rules. When I came home from school, Hugo would make a polite attempt at conversation, such as, "*Bonjour,* Eric. How was school today?"

Depending on my mood, I would answer under my breath either *"Bon"*—fine—or "Why do you care?"

No matter what I said, as the grown-up, he could accuse

me of being rude in my response. An unsatisfactory answer was a big enough offense that Hugo could pick a fight with me, though he had to be careful in his attacks: my mother's rule was that Hugo couldn't physically discipline me. Since he wasn't allowed to beat me, he sought subtle ways to push me around and make sure that I knew who was boss.

"You little brat," he often began. "I am the man in the house and you need to show me some respect."

Respect was the name of the game and a lack of respect was cause for him to get aggressive: nothing too overt, just a shove, a push, a pinch.

On my way into the kitchen, I sometimes threw my book bag on the sofa instead of putting it away in my room, which was enough cause for Hugo to open my bag and start throwing my books around, telling me to "shape up and stop being such a freaking slob." He would throw a tantrum over the mess and claim to be doing it as an advocate of my mother. "Your mother works so hard, Eric! When she comes home, she doesn't have the time or the energy to clean up after you. Show her some goddamn respect and put away your shit."

He could, if he chose—and it was all his choice—put his hand on my shoulder and push me into the wall like the bigger kids did at school, quick and rough before the teachers could catch them. "You go to school to learn, you little bum," he might say, pounding me with a book. "Did you learn anything today or did you do the teaching? Lessons in how to be a dis-respectful little beast, perhaps?"

When Hugo wanted to drag the action out longer, he would ignore the book bag, and let me go into the kitchen to prepare my afternoon snack.

In France, *le goûter* is an important part of daily life. It might be a crêpe with caramel sauce or a baguette with a piece of chocolate smeared on it, Nutella-style. It could be a tartine with *chèvre frais* and olives or with raspberries and cream cheese.

I loved food, and so my *goûter* was as precious to me as cellphones are to kids today. I dreamed about my *goûter*. I spent most of Sunday thinking about my *goûter* for the week. My mother shopped for me especially so that I might have everything that I needed to tide me over until dinner.

But I was also a bit of a glutton and chances were good that unsupervised by my mother, I would eat much more than a snack. This was another opportunity for Hugo to reprimand me. So he watched me as I assembled the ingredients of what I would eat that day. I reached for the baguette, the butter, the Nutella, the raspberries. There was a knife, a plate, a napkin.

If he was in a good mood, Hugo would watch me assemble my snack and be sated by the fact that as I spread Nutella on the bread, I was visibly agitated. By this point I was usually ready to enter the fight. I wanted an excuse to tell him off, to speak disrespectfully, to tell him what I really thought of him.

If he was in a slightly less favorable mood, he had many ways he could toy with me, such as knocking the bread off the plate, then demanding that I pick it up. "Stop being so clumsy, Eric." Or, if there was jam out, he would pour it out on the floor, telling me to clean up the mess—this was a favorite tactic.

No matter what I did, I was vulnerable, and Hugo liked it that way. I was only seven and it would take me a long time—years—to gain the height and the courage to stand my ground and dare to fight back.

Hugo was patient in his cruelty. He trained me to mistrust him and even hate him, the way one might train a dog to fight.

I learned to heel to his commands, and my senses developed so that soon I could read the signs and respond to the danger at hand.

. What was harder to learn, what would take decades and putting an ocean between me and the man who dared to call himself my second father, was how to manage the anger. It just grew and grew inside of me. It became one of my coldest comforts: imagining all of the ways in which I would get back at Hugo and anyone else who dared to test me when I was bigger and stronger, away from my mother's house and free to defend myself.

5

::::

Out of the Pot and into the Frying Pan

Although my mother never asked me what was going on with Hugo, she noticed that I was changing. I was increasingly isolated at school, while at home I was more aggressive. The only way that I could tell she was sorry for all of the changes in our lives was through her food. Cooking gave her emotions a place to go.

As soon as I woke up, I went to the kitchen, where she had begun preparing dinner before she left for work. She indulged my increasingly specific requests—roasted capon with black olives, leg of lamb English-style, roast pork with mustard—and spoiled me with elaborate recipes from the nouvelle cuisine cookbooks on her bedside table.

The trips that we planned to restaurants became more elaborate too. In the beginning, she and Hugo sought out the best restaurants in the village, then the region. Soon, we were driving hours to Michelin-starred destinations like Café de la Paix, La Baumanière, Negresco, and Michel Guèrard. I had my special restaurant suit, and spent weeks looking forward to the afternoons when I'd be presented with the *chariot de dessert*, the old-fashioned dessert cart, and allowed to choose as many pastries as I wanted.

There was always excitement around the trip—choosing the restaurants from the guides (Michelin or Gault et Millau), and taking recommendations from friends. My mother, Hugo, and I would talk about it for weeks before. My mother would clip articles about great chefs and restaurants for me to read alongside the cookbooks that I devoured before bed. For me, the biggest thrills at these restaurants, besides the food, were the ritual and the formality. The white tablecloths were always starched and set with precision. Water was never dumped into a glass; it was poured with a certain style. When Hugo ordered wine, they brought out special glasses and decanted the bottle just so. Duck was carved tableside, crèpes were flambéed before our eyes. It was a magnificent performance and I relished every second of it.

The waiters were always respectful to me. Even though I was wide-eyed and impressed by their every gesture, they could tell that I was knowledgeable about food. I'd read from my own menu and say, "I'm going to try the rack of lamb stuffed with truffles, please." No one ever offered me anything akin to a kid's menu; I'm not sure such a thing even existed in France back then.

The biggest revelation occurred at Negresco, a decadent

restaurant in Nice. The chef, Jacques Maximin, used the southern ingredients that I loved and really knew how to enhance their flavors, like a stuffed zucchini flower *nappéd* with a truffle sauce that had me begging for more, or a *chiboust aux fraises des bois,* a light-as-air cream pastry studded with fresh wild strawberries. After the meal, I announced to my proud mother that I'd never tasted anything so good in my life.

"The little prince has royal tastes," Hugo grumbled. But I didn't care. A great meal was always the best medicine for the wound that he was in my life.

Hugo occasionally helped out around the house and at my mother's stores, but what he really excelled at was spending her money and bossing me around. When my mother got pregnant, his bullying only intensified. With my mother in a more delicate condition, I had to fend for myself. She made sure that he bought the *jambon de Paris* and cakes and yogurts that I loved for my after-school snack, but Hugo would hide them from me. I could never convince her that I couldn't find them in the fridge.

While my mother was pregnant, she found out that Hugo had been cheating on her, and she kicked him out with a fury I'd never seen.

The next night, he returned and pleaded with her to take him back, saying he couldn't live without her, he'd never do it again, he just couldn't bear her being confined to bed without being able to touch her, and so on and so forth. She yelled at him to get out, that he was a lowlife, a sponge, and, to top it off, a lousy lover. Before I knew what was happening, he grabbed a pair of manicure scissors and slit his wrists right in front of us.

"You have to keep him, Maman," I pleaded, traumatized, as his blood spurted into the bathroom sink and all over the floor.

I had never seen anything like it. There was so much blood, I was certain that if I didn't act quickly, Hugo would die. I thought I hated him, but I didn't want to watch him die.

"Look what you've done!" I yelled at my mother. "What will happen to the baby? Who will look after me while you work? You can't just kick him out in the street."

Just like Hugo, I was crying and begging her to take mercy on him for the sake of the "family."

"You want him to stay?" my mother asked, incredulous.

"Yes," I insisted.

"Then he can stay," my mother said, her face drained and exhausted. Then she turned around and went back to bed.

And so I saved him. Later on, my mother told me that the bastard had known exactly how to cut himself without slicing an artery. I could hardly believe it: it had all been a show.

Soon after Hugo's "suicide attempt," my little sister, Marika, was born. Then, one weekend when I was away visiting my father, my mother and Hugo got married and his place in our home was cemented. Hugo used Marika as a wedge to try and drive me out of the family. "Now," he would remind me, "you are the bastard in the house." He humiliated me whenever he could, insulting me in front of other people. When we were home alone, it became increasingly physical. I began to fight him as hard as I could, knowing that even if he was bigger than I was, I could outsmart him and push him to his limit. What I didn't realize was that I was the one on the edge.

• • •

"Eric, clear the dishes," Hugo barked one night after I'd finished the last of the *millefeuille à la vanille.*

"Absolutely not."

"No TV then," he said.

"Bullshit!" I yelled.

I calmly went to my room and locked the door. He banged on it for what must have been twenty minutes. My mother tried for ten more, telling me to grow up and open the door. But I wouldn't give in. Instead I started writing notes and folding them into elaborate little envelopes I made using my art paper from class.

"Je vous dis merde!" read the first.

"You're all assholes!" said another.

"Go fuck yourselves!" was my final shot.

I knew that there would be hell to pay when I finally opened the door. My mother would get the belt, in an attempt to discipline me, but that only made me want to challenge her more. If I was going to be beaten, I was going to make sure they knew exactly how I felt about them before the first blow. *Go fuck yourselves.* I couldn't say the words. I couldn't fight back physically. But scribbling the curses, whispering them as I wrote, a feeling of pride bloomed in my chest. I wasn't just taking it—I was standing up for myself, on paper, if nowhere else. *You're all assholes!*

The pounding on the door intensified and Marika cried louder. My mother threatened everything she could think of, from a ban on desserts to no more visits to my father, but I wouldn't turn the lock. After they gave up and went to bed, I blasted my clock radio and sang Michel Sardou and Johnny Hallyday at the top of my lungs until it was almost lights out.

The immediate backlash wasn't that bad, but one night a

few weeks later, my mother told me that she wanted me to
"get a better education." She handed me a brochure showing
kids my age wearing military uniforms in front of a château.

"But I always get very good grades!" I protested.

"It's the best school. You can learn horseback riding. You
get to wear a beautiful uniform. You'll even have your own
room!" She made it sound like Club Med. Finally, she arrived
at the real reason: "You have to learn discipline and respect.
We can't control you anymore."

I didn't understand who this "we" was. She was the one in
charge of discipline; Hugo wasn't allowed to touch me (at least
not in front of her), but by that point I had become desensi-
tized to her punishment. She would hit me with a belt, and I'd
just laugh and say, "What are you doing? I can't feel anything."
Or, "Ha-ha! That tickles!" She would get so furious she'd go to
her room and cry.

"I'll go live with my father then," I said. "He wants me to
be with him." I wasn't sure about this, but in that moment I
needed him to rescue me.

"He's married to Francine now, Eric, and you know she
doesn't want you around," was her reply. "The last time you
came back from their house, she didn't even bother to fold
your clothes before shoving them in your suitcase. Besides,
you don't want to have to eat her food every day, do you? This
is for the best. Anyway, you don't have a choice. You're already
enrolled. Classes start after New Year's."

"But the school year has just started! I can behave, I promise." It was suddenly clear how desperately serious the situation had become.

My mother glared at me. "Maybe you should have thought
about that when you were making our lives so impossible."

I called my father in the hopes that he might save me from this fate. I don't know what I expected him to say, but I didn't expect him to ship me off without trying, like my mother had.

"I'm sorry, Eric, but I can't take you," he said, apologetic but firm. "Your mother says you need discipline and values, and this is the only way you'll learn. She doesn't know how to control you anymore. I'll see you in the summer. Maybe you can come to visit one weekend."

Eight years old, I thought, *and thrown away.*

6

∷

Boarding School

My mother and Hugo put my suitcase in the trunk of their new car, strapped Marika in, and drove us two and a half hours to Perpignan, a small city on the southernmost tip of France. Boys were running between arches in the courtyard of a building that looked about fifty thousand years old, and they weren't wearing fancy uniforms: this wasn't the military academy I'd seen in the brochure. My mother hadn't been able to get me enrolled at the academy after all, so she was sending me to Saint Louis de Gonzague, a Catholic school with the reputation for having, as my mom put it, "the best education."

"All of the foreign presidents and diplomats send their

sons here," she said with pride, as though this could possibly matter to me.

Only a heartless woman would send her eight-year-old away to school, I thought, with the kind of venom I usually reserved for Hugo.

The second-floor dormitory with its spare, military barrack–style bunk beds gave a hint of the grim school year ahead of me. My mother was suddenly emotional and I could see in her face that she knew she had made a mistake. When she moved to hug me goodbye, I turned away from her embrace. She leaned in to kiss my cheek and I turned away from that too. My mother winced, as if the gesture physically hurt; then she put on her "it's for the best, *chéri*" smile.

Hugo gave me a victorious pat, and that was it. They drove off with Marika sleeping in the backseat. I refused to even raise my hand and wave.

There were no private rooms at Saint Louis de Gonzague, just a drafty dormitory where forty boys slept in narrow iron beds, shared a single shower, and pissed in a trough. At this point in my (short) life, I was used to abrupt transitions and having to start over in a new place. But the first night in my tiny bed, I felt as if loneliness had tied itself around my ankle like an anchor with a knot that I would never untangle. I tried to pretend that it was summer and I was in my grandfather's apricot tree at their house in Cagnes-sur-Mer, missing home but enjoying my independence. But the cold, hard bunk was no substitute for the tree that was my summertime friend.

When class began, it was clear that I was far ahead in my lessons, so I decided it wasn't worth it to pay attention to the lady with the gray chignon at the front of the class. During the afternoon study period, there was nothing for me to study, so I read comic books. Finally, someone noticed: after six weeks or so, the school asked for my mother's permission to advance me from second to third grade. She said yes without asking me, proud to be the parent of a genius.

Suddenly I was dropped into a new group of boys who knew things I didn't, such as the basics of math and grammar. (And in France, if you don't know grammar, you're finished.) My new teacher couldn't be bothered to bring me up to speed, never mind take the time to answer my questions about politics and current events. In a single week, I went from being far ahead of my classmates to barely keeping up to falling behind.

I spent more and more time in the courtyard, halfheartedly playing with different groups of boys, because study hall had become torturous: I knew that I couldn't catch up to my new classmates. There was none of the usual comfort that I found in the food. It was cheap and disgusting, overcooked rice with raw garlic being a staple. I'd never known truly bad food before, and the comedown was dramatic.

On the occasional longed-for weekend when someone would come get me, I'd spend Saturday alone with Hugo and Marika while my mother worked; on a Sunday we might go on an outing—a picnic or fishing—before I was driven back to school, where no comforts or friends awaited me. My aunt Janine occasionally brought me back to Montpellier. My father never did invite me to visit.

My grades started to slip, then fail. During recess and study hall, where I spent most of my time, the man I'll call Père Damien, the former priest in charge of us during those hours, began paying more attention to me. In the early 1970s, a priest who had been forced to resign was considered *défroqué*—defrocked. You were shamed, but not fired, because the Church was very protective of itself and its own. Instead, defrocked priests were simply moved to another post. I would soon learn why Père Damien had lost his collar.

He must've seen how disengaged I'd become from the other boys, so he would often talk to me, staying with me after the other kids had gone back to the dorm. Once I'd told him all about how my mother and Hugo had conspired to send me away and wouldn't even come get me on weekends, he said that he would ask my mother's permission to take me around town when I wasn't back home. She happily arranged to pay him for these outings, which I looked forward to all week.

I'd always wanted an older brother, and Père Damien, with his American-style clothes and friendly manner, seemed to fit the bill. We'd walk into town to see a movie, or go to a flea market and look at old books and toys. We talked about grown-up things, mainly about my parents and their divorce, and how much I hated school. I also got to ask him the questions I had about religion. I was puzzled by Catholic rituals (my aunt Monique took me to mass in Nîmes, but I was only interested in how to get the cookie that they served at the end) and suspicious about origin stories like Adam and Eve. Though mysterious, Père Damien was warm and kind and always asked the right questions. He soon got me to open up. I felt like there was at least one person in Perpignan who understood me.

Sometimes he'd take me along as he ran errands to the stationery shop or the local market. On Saturdays, there was a flea market adjacent to the school and I began to accompany him as he shopped and talked to the merchants. A few weeks into our friendship, he took me to a part of town I'd never visited before. He told me to wait in the street for a few minutes while he ran an errand. I watched him go into a store with neon silhouettes and racy photos of curvy women on the curtained window. When he returned to my side five minutes later, he took my hand and walked me back to school.

The following weekend, after we'd gone to the Saturday flea market, Père Damien invited me to his room to watch TV. He hung his overcoat on the back of the door. Underneath he was wearing a cardigan and old work pants, which reminded me of my grandfather. There was barely space in his room for his monk-size bed. In order to watch the tiny set propped on his desk, we had to sit side by side on Père Damien's bed.

A few minutes into the show, he turned down the volume. "How do you do it with your mom and dad?" he asked me.

"What do you mean?"

"I mean, when they give you kisses and caresses."

I froze. "They don't give me kisses and caresses."

"Sure they do." He practically purred the words and I could feel a wave of panic washing over me.

"They really don't," I insisted.

Père Damien turned the volume back up, but he moved closer to me. During a commercial, he began stroking my arm. I stared at the set, pretending to be interested in the shampoo the woman was advertising. He leaned over to kiss my neck, his long hair falling around his face and onto my stomach.

"My dad doesn't do that," I said, pushing him away.

"Oh, but you know he would love to give you affection. I know for a fact that he'd love to do that to you. Let me show you. . . ."

"No!" I was uncomfortable, and suddenly angry that Père Damien would try to take my father's place, or even pretend to know what he was like. "You're not my dad, and I don't want you to do that. Leave me alone. I want to get out of here."

I got up and left, shutting the door. I was so scared that he would run after me. In my stomach I could sense that something wrong had just happened, and there was only one person who could help prevent it from happening again. I hurried to the phone booth to call my mother, looking over my shoulder to make sure he wasn't coming. I was terrified by what he would do if he caught me. Within moments, my only friend had become my enemy.

"What's going on?" my mother asked, sounding surprised to hear from me. It was dinnertime back home, and I could hear Marika crying in the background.

"We were watching TV and he said he wanted to give me affection like Dad and he started to kiss—"

"Who's 'we'?" she asked, sounding simultaneously concerned and annoyed.

"Père Damien," I whispered into the receiver. There were other boys around, and I didn't want them to hear what I was telling my mother. "He's acting weird."

I could hear the sharp intake of her breath and could picture the mixture of anger and aggression on her face. There was nothing quite like my mother in mama-bear mode. I knew that Père Damien was going to lose a limb, or his job, or both.

"I will call you back," my mother said. "Go to your dorm and don't talk to anyone."

"I don't want to be here anymore, Mom," I said, my toughness temporarily failing me. "I want to come home."

I forced myself to go to dinner, sitting away from the other boys. I was disturbed in a way I couldn't put into words. I slept that night with a kind of fear that I had never known. After all of the bad things I had seen and felt in my life so far, it was a terrible feeling to realize that there were even more horrible things out there, waiting to make themselves known. But not knowing what they were yet meant that I could not prepare myself, and the mixture of fear and helplessness was crippling.

The next day, one of the teachers found me in the courtyard and led me down the hallway to wait for my mother, who was in the head priest's office.

When she came out, her dark eyes shining, she said, "It's not going to happen again. And we'll get you out of here."

"Should I pack?"

Her eyes softened for a moment. "You can't come home until the end of the year," she said. "You have to finish the semester. I'm so sorry, my love." She held me for a minute, then pulled away, saying she had a long drive home.

The next day in study hall, I was terrified at the prospect of facing him again. I halfheartedly goofed around with the kid next to me to try to cover up my fear. Suddenly, Père Damien banged on my old hinge-top desk so hard it rattled the pencils and rulers inside.

"Get to work, Ripert!" he yelled. "Maybe if you studied harder you'd have better grades."

The other boys laughed, and I dove into my homework, furious and confused.

After everyone had left, I told myself to be brave, even though I was shaking, and I went up to Père Damien to ask him why he was picking on me.

"I can't believe you said all that to your mother!" he hissed. "You know I'm not allowed to talk to you again."

"I thought you were my friend," I said.

"Never," he spat. "You spoiled rich kids are all the same. Tell your mother to buy you a new friend."

For the rest of the year, whenever I saw Père Damien alone with other kids, my stomach tightened with fear, sensing that he might try to kiss them in his little room too. What he had done was wrong, but apparently it wasn't wrong enough to get him fired, or wrong enough for my mother to take me out of school. When I stole the Pagnol from my mother's house, she had admonished me to be someone she could trust. I tried to be trustworthy. Even that second-rate drama queen Hugo could trust me to have his back when the going got rough. But whom could I trust? *No one,* I thought. No one.

I got through the last few months of that school year like a prisoner who knows that he will soon be paroled, if he can just keep his head up. I made myself anticipate the bright green smell of basil as I walked to the market with my grandma Maguy. I dreamed of long afternoons spent in the apricot tree, reading books borrowed from the nearby library. There would be Sunday lunches with the Italian cousins, and then I'd be off to Nîmes where my aunt Monique would spoil me beyond her means and my cousin Patrick would be the brother I never had. I thought about the jazz records my father would play when he came home from the bank during our weeks together, asking me what I thought about Mingus or Bird while we went down into his cellar to top off his vinegar barrel with the half-empty wine bottles from the party the weekend before. I collected my memories like the coins I sometimes found on the beach: shiny valuable things hidden by piles and piles of sand.

On the last day of school, when my mother came to pick me up, she hugged me and in her embrace, I could feel a hundred apologies. But I let my arms hang loosely by my sides. I did not—would not—hug her back.

7

Paper Airplanes

October 2, 1975

Dear Eric,

I have just seen the most incredible boxing match on TV. They called it the "Thriller in Manila." Two Americans. Muhammad Ali and Joe Frazier. Ali has a face like a baby, but he took Frazier out in 14 sizzling rounds.

Ali calls himself the greatest and I must tell you, some people call him cocky, but I like it. Be confident, Eric. Be cocky if you feel like it. We only get one shot at this life, so why not float like a butterfly and sting like a bee?

All my love,
The Greatest Papa, Me

By the time I was nine, the suitcase underneath my bed was filled with letters from my father, but I never wrote him back. It wasn't my thing. Still, I loved getting his letters. They whizzed into my quiet and disconnected life like paper airplanes from a faraway land.

Before Hugo appeared on the scene, I did not mind all the ways my mother tried to pull me close. She picked my clothes, brushed my hair, hugged me on the steps of the school, and cupped my face with both hands when she kissed me, one kiss for each cheek, before I fell asleep at night.

I knew from watching the boys at school that a certain amount of exasperated pulling away was built in to the part that I had to play—the role of the beloved son whose mother cannot face that he is no longer a little baby.

But after Hugo, my pulling away was no act. My mother had, to my mind, chosen poorly, and I strove to remind her of this failing on a daily basis. Whenever she hugged me, whenever she kissed me, I wrestled away with a force that I hoped would convey the depth of my disappointment.

It was a round robin of pain and heartbreak: My father broke my mother's heart. My mother broke my heart by marrying Hugo. Hugo punished me because my mother was no longer happy with him and I hated him in return.

Even my father, married now to Francine and with another baby on the way, could not escape the fury that swirled around our home. Once, when driving me home after a holiday, he bought something in her store—a pair of pants, a belt—I suppose as a way to make amends. But she hated him as much as I idolized him, and as soon as he pulled away from the curb, she started in.

"Only hicks drive Audis," she'd sniff. "And did you see the

pants he was wearing? Ridiculous. And his glasses are from 1965. I mean, not only is he cheap, the man has no taste. What a *paysan*."

Anytime I mentioned my father—after I'd read and re-read one of his letters or talked about how excited I was to spend vacation with him—she'd rip him apart. He was a boring *fonctionnaire*, a paper-pusher in an unfashionable suit. He never wanted the beautiful things that she was working so hard to provide for us. He was a crappy trumpet player, a pathetic dresser, a cheat.

But nothing she said could temper the love that I had for my father. He was a big personality, a bon vivant, and an entertainer, but he was also unabashed and generous in his affection. My mother tried to impress me. All throughout my childhood, she worked hard to give me the best. She took me on trips to Paris when she was shopping for her boutique, she took me to fancy restaurants and bought me fancy clothes. She always let me know that everything we owned, from our car to the food on our plates, was *"le top."* But that was the difference between my mother and my father: my father might not have been the best dresser, might have worked in his garden in an old stained T-shirt, and might have gone too far when he puffed out his cheeks to play the trumpet like Louis Armstrong, but there was never any mistaking his love for me. When I walked into the room, his eyes lit up and he wrapped me in his arms as if it was Christmas morning and I was the best gift imaginable.

My mother was my caregiver, the one I depended on. Day in and day out, she did what my father had to do only on the occasional weekend visit and summer vacation. But her love didn't seem to be as big or as boisterous. It wasn't her fault, but it was her fate, like so many single mothers, to be caught between a wistful child and his fantasies of the father who is perfect, in part because he is hardly ever there.

The summer after I returned from boarding school, I spent a few weeks with my father. He took me to the beach for the day, just me and him, no Francine, which was a gift in and of itself. My father sat on the shore reading a book and drinking pastis. I played in the sand just a few yards away, spending the afternoon making the most elaborate sand castles. I used every tool at my disposal—buckets, shovels, twigs—and it took me hours to build. Then, when I was nearly done, a kid came by and kicked it down, stomping on it left and right.

I went crying to my father and he looked over at the kid I pointed out. My father stood up, furious, and said, "Eric, you have to go over there and teach that kid a lesson. I want you to go down there and kick his ass."

With that he pushed me forward, toward the water's edge where the kid was playing in the waves. My father was watching me closely—every time I turned, he was there—making sure that I would accomplish this task of defending myself.

I got to the kid and tapped him on his shoulder.

"What do you want?" the kid sneered, turning his back to me. In that moment, I knew that he did not live with a bully like Hugo, because he did not seem to know that you never, never turn your back on your opponent. Without hesitation, I jumped onto his back and he fell onto the sand. He was so startled that he couldn't regain ground as I straddled him, pummeling him with my fists.

The kid's father came running down to the water's edge, followed swiftly by my father. The boy's father reached for me, yelling, "Hey, get off my son!"

My father grabbed his hand and said, "Well, tell your son this is what he gets for kicking over other kids' sand castles."

The two men began to argue, and feeling the confidence of having my father close, I lit into the boy even harder. I hadn't wanted to fight him, but now I could feel the pleasure of holding him down and beating him. I did not beat him as a proxy for Hugo; I didn't imagine that I would one day punch Hugo the way I punched this boy. Rather, I beat him the way I had learned from being the recipient of Hugo's bullying and it frightened me, more than a little, how much it pleased me to pummel him, to lose control.

8

::::

Maguy

Summers were a welcome reprieve, not because I liked being out of school, but because I knew that this was my time to escape Hugo. Each summer, I went first to Nice to spend a few weeks with my maternal grandfather, then to Nîmes to spend a few weeks with my father's side of the family. They were all excellent cooks.

My mother's mother, Marthe, died of breast cancer when my mother was sixteen. My grandfather was devastated and completely overwhelmed. It was the late 1950s and he didn't know how to manage as a single father. My mother's older brother had Down syndrome and required nearly round-the-clock care. So, in a move that was shocking at the time, my grandfather went to a local dating agency to find a wife, and quickly. He was introduced right away to Maguy, a divorcee with a young son of her own. The two got along well and soon agreed that a quick marriage was both the most practical and respectable way to proceed.

Maguy was blond, pretty, warm, kind, and generous to the core. She came from a big Italian family and soon all of her siblings and their extended families became part of our family too. Maguy mended clothes for a living in the basement of their simple stucco home in Cagnes-sur-Mer. She sewed a few feet away from the workshop where my grandfather repaired televisions and tinkered with his homemade shortwave radio.

Maguy raised my uncle Roger as if he were her own son. Looking back, I can see how much she taught me about hard work and how to carry oneself with quiet dignity around difficult people like my grandfather, who made his demands very clearly known, but rarely his affection. Their marriage worked because Maguy could tell, from the start, how much heart my grandfather had, and she never lost sight of this.

Maguy also taught me how food brings people together, and how it also has the power to make even the loneliest person feel like the center of the universe. From the moment I arrived each summer, Maguy would bombard me with a steady parade of my favorite dishes. *Pissaladière. Ravioli de daube. Paupiette de veau* with fresh peas. *"Manges! Manges!"* she would say, which, in her faint Italian accent, always sounded like *"Mangia! Mangia!"* This was not the elegant food of my mother's kitchen—no *saumon en croûte* or *dacquoises* in Maguy's house. This was simple food, cooked from the heart. I loved nothing more.

At my grandparents' house, I was still a loner and a troublemaker. I'd climb the apricot tree in the yard and spend hours hidden in its canopy, daydreaming about having my family together again in our old house in St. Tropez, with its little garden and henhouse. The tree felt safe (and its fruit was delicious). When I was on the ground, I busied myself figuring out ways to destroy the well-kept garden around me. I'd make dams out of dirt, fill the centers with the hose, then kick in one side and watch as the muddy water flooded the *pétanque* field down the hill. I'd roll my grandfather's old tires in the mud and chase them into the street. I'd pick every lemon, yellow or green, from the tree, and pretend they were grenades. I'd tear the wings off of flies and drown ants in water. My grandparents called me "turbulent" or hyper, and *"espiègle,"* mischievous. When I was being especially bad, my grandfather would grab me with his rough hands and yell, "You have the devil in your body! I have a secret medicine to get it out!" Then he'd spank me and send me to my room. But for me, being left to my imagination never felt like punishment. Quite the opposite—it was where I preferred to be.

Partly to keep me out of trouble and partly because she could tell how much I loved it, Maguy would hand me my own wicker basket every morning and take me with her to the market. For me, our shopping trips were more about the smells than the produce we brought back up the hill. By the summer of my sixth year, I was so attuned to the scents of the market that I could have found my way through our shopping list blindfolded. To start, I would let the scent of *pains au chocolat* ready to come out of the oven guide me to the bakery. I could smell they were ready before I could see them, and that was a kind of training for my future career too: being able to tell, from a room away, the exact moment when the chocolate began to crisp as it overflowed the golden pastries at the edges. Next I would follow the metallic odor of blood to the butcher across the street where we bought veal and beef. After that I sought out the fustiness of the aged ham and sausage at the charcuterie, and then the grocer, where barrels of briny-slick olives pricked the back of my nostrils. Finally, baskets already heavy, we would make our way to the covered market, where every scent was even more intensified by the incubator effect of the hot metal roof.

The top note of the market's bouquet was always basil, bright and vibrant, a sunny green perfume. To this day, basil never fails to trigger a palpable swell of joy in my chest. I almost swooned at the fragrance of anise, clove, and mint coming from the hundreds of foot-tall bunches jammed into beat-up cans of water. I followed Maguy closely as she picked her way through stacks of salted baccalau; piles of papery, honey-scented zucchini blossoms that seemed to float, one on top of the other; booths manned by farmers who tried to sweet-talk us into looking at their goods, their tables sagging under the weight of musky-sweet melons. Even the zucchini had their own slightly bitter perfume. Peppers, capers, anchovies, tomatoes, goat cheese, grassy olive oil: all the brawny, fragrant flavors of Provence vied for my attention.

Though sweet and friendly, Maguy wasn't the easy mark vendors often took her for. She insisted on the best quality and price. "These tomatoes aren't ripe," she would say, pressing her finger to the unyielding flesh and giving it an accusatory sniff before putting it back. "The bread had a better crust yesterday," she would tell the baker.

"Smell this melon, Eric," she would say, bringing my nose to the stem end. "It smells like rotting papaya. That means it's too ripe. And look: bigger dimples mean female melons, which means they're sweeter. *Tu comprends?*"

Everything was touched, inhaled, disputed. And since she was always smiling, she always got what she wanted. If I was good, Maguy would give me a few francs and let me buy whatever I wanted. Inevitably, I chose a pastry.

Back home, I'd watch as Maguy sorted the produce, leaving most of it in a basket outside the back door, French country-style, and tied on her apron. Then she started making *ratatouille* or *petit farci* or *gigot d'agneau*—rustic dishes that filled the small, white-tiled kitchen with their slow-simmering odors. Except for a few pizza-making classes she'd taken from a local housewife, Maguy was self-taught. She was an intuitive cook. She knew how to work with her hands and season instinctively.

When she made *petit farci*, she'd seek out the best tomatoes she could find, neatly hollowing them out and setting aside any usable scraps. Then she'd mince the *jambon de Paris*, veal, and pork (and maybe a little diced coppa) by hand in one of her bowls, her fingers telling her if the mixture was too coarse or too soft. Next she'd stir in the *herbes de Provence* I'd gathered from the backyard, along with some parsley and nutmeg, and add an egg. Every time, without using a single measuring cup or spoon, she would have just enough to fill the vegetables, without a speck left over. Her senses were a steady, reliable guide.

Of all of the food I ate during those summers, there was one dish that I willed into being every day: Maguy's *tarte aux pommes*. The scent of butter and apple was sunshine itself. I loved it so much, she made one for me every day, no matter how much it heated up the already-broiling kitchen. I watched her prepare the dough in the afternoon, rolling it impossibly thin and laying it on a battered old baking sheet. Her secret was using *demi-sel* (salted) butter instead of unsalted, to enhance the sweetness of the apples. Then, she covered the dough with a kitchen towel and put it in the refrigerator to harden overnight. During my nap, she would pull out the dough from the day before, layer translucent apple slivers over the pricked crust, sprinkle a few teaspoons of sugar on top, and pop it in the oven. That was all. No fancy techniques, no sticky glaze, and no comparison. I could never wait for it to cool. Even though Maguy insisted that I share, all twelve thin, crisp, just-sweet rectangular slices were gone within minutes.

Although Maguy turned out the same dishes that were being made all over the south of France at the time, her food contained the most essential ingredient: love. True, the quality of her meals was due in part to the quality of the produce she used. (Even today, with access to the best produce in America, I will never be able to buy a tomato or an eggplant that tastes as intensely itself as those Maguy got in her village from the truck farmers she knew by name.) But what truly made the difference was that she put her feelings for her family into every pot. She cooked with the same care and attention that she gave everyone in her orbit. Every dish tasted as though it was made just for me.

And, in a way, it was. Maguy wasn't interested in getting me to help. Men, I was constantly reminded, had no place in the kitchen. *"T'es toujours dans mes jupons dans la cuisine!"* I was told in every house: You're always in my skirts in the kitchen! But watching from her doorway was all the experience I needed. Other kids looked to TV to entertain and instruct them; I had a view of my grandmother's stove.

Sunday was my favorite day in Cagnes-sur-Mer. I'd climb the apricot tree and perch in my special forked branch, my hands smelling of bark and verbena. If I sat facing the house, I could look through the balcony's iron bars and catch a glimpse of Maguy in her kitchen, busier than usual. If I turned the other way, I could see the château on top of the hill across the valley. Many of my daydreams took place in that castle. I'd swing across the moat, narrowly avoiding the alligators, to face off a gang of cowboys and knights. My heroic fantasies always culminated in somehow bringing my parents back together again. My longing for them was almost physical: when I was with one, I felt the absence of the other like a dull ache. And when I was on my own like this, I missed them both even more. Like some people are tired all the time, I was in a constant state of missing my mother and father. But Sunday lunch made things better, if only for the afternoon.

Sunday mornings, I would watch as my grandfather and his brother-in-law Gaston hauled the long wooden table out to the yard below and set it up with at least twenty mismatched folding chairs in preparation for Maguy's big, boisterous Italian family, who came for lunch and games every week. Even from up in the tree, I could sense the excitement building in the house, which would burst forth as soon as the first old Renault chugged up the steep driveway, followed by the second, third . . . sixth. . . . By then I was out of hiding, ready to be pinched and hugged—and fed.

The house and yard filled with people, laughter, and food. The women always gathered upstairs around the dining room table to roll out tagliatelle on a wooden board, or stamp out ravioli and fill them with cheese while a big pot of Bolognese sauce simmered on the stove in the kitchen. Meanwhile, the

men had their first aperitif, always pastis or pernod, and divided into teams to play *pétanque*. The brightly colored metal
balls thudded on the sand court. The young cousins peeled off
and attacked the foosball table in the basement. Then we'd
play other games: I'd put on my Zorro outfit and run through
the garden with them, tearing out *verveine*, mint, and rosemary by the handful as we raced past the bushes to see how
much we could collect before my grandfather got mad at us
for ruining his plants.

But as much as I liked playing with the other kids, I preferred to be with the adults. To be specific, I wanted nothing
more than for the women to teach me how to roll out pasta
and then hang it to dry on an old broomstick. When I tried to
watch, they just ruffled my hair and told me to keep out of the
way. "Go play with the boys!" they'd say, chasing me away with
a pat and a shake of their heads before returning to their good-
natured gossip.

By two o'clock, all twenty of us were crammed around the
rickety table in the front yard. I usually ended up squeezed
between adults, listening to them argue about leftist politics.
There were always the heated discussions about who cheated
at *pétanque* or cards, who caught the biggest octopus the last
time they went diving, and who made the best *soupe de poisson* over a campfire on the beach at Triasse.

It was a roller coaster of intensity: the euphoria of the
games followed by the drama of who won, who lost, who
cheated. All of the men pretended to be angry after the game
and no one was more moody about the outcome than my
grandfather, whom everyone allowed to win, so that the head
of the household would be satisfied and not ruin the day.

Bowls of fresh pasta and platters of vegetables that Maguy

and I had chosen at the market that morning were washed down with bottles of rough wine. People didn't speak; they yelled. But it was all warm and loving, filled with hugs and the pure satisfaction of coming together around the table for an afternoon. There was incredible solidarity among Maguy's family: because of the economic crisis in Italy, everyone pooled their money to send relatives sugar, coffee, clothes, whatever they lacked. And even though my grandfather didn't know how to express his love as easily as they did, everyone understood that underneath his gruffness, he loved us all. For a handful of Sundays a year, I felt like part of a real family.

After a few weeks with my mother's family, I was sent off by train to Nîmes, a few hours away, for the next stop on my summer vacation.

The first few days of my visit were spent with my father's parents in the old part of town. My grandfather would take me to the railway-pensioner garden to harvest dinner, spending hours chatting with other retired train workers. In the big cities, every employee of the railroad was given a large plot of land to farm. The size of the parcel depended on how long you worked for the railroad and what position you held, but it was yours to cultivate however you liked. My grandfather's garden was about two thousand square feet with a little shack. It was a great benefit, and my grandfather tended it with pride and pleasure.

At home, I watched my grandmother Emilienne can tomatoes, cook down plums for jam, and put up jars of cherries or apricots in brandy. She made me endless *croque monsieurs* using a medieval-looking iron contraption that clamped the bread between long handles so you could hold it over a fire to make melty, lightly charred sandwiches. (After she passed away in 1998, I honored her with a dish at Le Bernardin. Granted, my *croque* was made with caviar and smoked salmon instead of ham and cheese, but I sought to imitate her golden crust, and the adoration and respect that went into it were entirely for her.)

After living like a retiree with my grandparents, I was ready to play with my cousins in deepest Provence. My cousins, aunt, and uncle lived modestly in a steeply A-framed cabin that my aunt Monique's husband built. Known in the Provençal dialect as a *mazé*, it was so small it almost seemed like a dollhouse, but I only slept there. Most of my time was spent running through the woods, hills, and vineyards with my cousin Patrick, who was about my age, and the kids from the few houses in the area.

Completely unsupervised out in the *garrigue*—the wild countryside of thyme, scrubby oak, and olive trees—Patrick and I ran free all day. We stripped the bark from trees, drowned ants in the inflatable pool, and played cowboys and Indians. We walked the mile into the village to buy baguettes, trying to catch a glimpse of the baker (we'd heard he kneaded the dough with his feet). We made up ghost stories in the woods after dark and sprinted home screaming our heads off. We even convinced ourselves that the Abominable Snowman was coming to get us—this in a place so hot that Patrick's father lay down on the table after lunch and turned the sprinkler on himself to stay cool while he napped.

It was the only time, as a child, that I can remember enjoying being with a group of kids my age. The games I had played in my imagination all those lonely afternoons in the back of my mother's store or up in the apricot tree in Cagnes-sur-Mer were finally brought to life with real characters. At the *mazé*, our gang made up new adventures all day long, living them out between meals, which were the only time we were separated or still. By the time we sat down to dinner, long after the late-August sun had set, Patrick and I were dirty, dusty, scraped, and tan.

At Monique's house, every afternoon had the excited, familial mood of Sunday lunch in Cagnes-sur-Mer. She'd line up a few wobbly folding tables under the welcome shade of some pine trees and we'd eat for hours. Patrick and I could run off and play and come back for seconds and thirds, and everyone would still be there, laughing and passing the platters. The cooking was simple and economical, served family-style on a plastic tablecloth. There was no room to turn around in that kitchen, let alone make anything sophisticated, but Monique took great pleasure in feeding her family tasty, satisfying meals.

The flavors of her dishes are ones that I can summon anytime, even now, forty years later: the basil brightening the flavor of the white beans in *soupe au pistou;* the salty sweetness of *pissaladière,* with its olives, onions, and anchovies on a flaky crust; the rich *fromage blanc* mixed with pungent anchovy cream and parsley that we slathered on toast; the garlicky brandade, the nature of which Monique debated with her bearlike brother-in-law Serge, who owned a restaurant near Montpellier. "No potato in the brandade!" Serge would yell, pounding on the table. "Just cod, two cloves of garlic, and olive oil!" Garlic, olive oil: the simple Provençal palate suited me.

When it came to eating, I was unstoppable. I didn't think twice about eating three or four croissants for breakfast, or the entire brick of cheese that Monique had bought the family for

the week. It never occurred to me that since Monique's husband was unemployed, they didn't have much money to spend
on food, or that I was supposed to share. My gluttony was a
running family joke. You couldn't tell it by looking at me because I was skinny and tall, but I could, and often did, eat everything in sight. Monique spoiled me by making my favorite
dishes, and liked to surprise me with a snack of hot buttered
pain de mie, toast that she grated chocolate over until it melted.

I could sense that my family wanted to please and protect
me. In the early 1970s, divorce was still taboo in Catholic
France, and Monique was as Catholic as they came. She knew
that as a result of my parents splitting up, I was now something
of an outsider in French society—divorce, to her, was a disaster. I wasn't living the life that an innocent child should. Years
later she told me that she felt a special duty to make sure I
knew I was loved and surrounded by family. She saw my sadness and did what she could to make me happy those few
weeks in the country: she cooked to mend my heart.

9

:::

Gone

"Eric, can I offer you a snack?" Hugo asked one afternoon when I got home from school. He sounded like he was reading from a script.

A snack? You've never given me a snack in your life, I thought. But I kept my mouth shut. There was, after all, food to be had.

Soon after I'd returned from boarding school, we moved to Foix, where I started the fifth grade in a one-room schoolhouse that was so old, we wrote with quills dipped into pots of ink. Then about a year later, my family moved to Andorra—a twenty-mile-wide sliver of a nation in the mountains between France and Spain—in a sudden and mysterious rush.

My mother explained that the French government taxed unfairly and that she'd be better off opening a store in a country that didn't charge sales tax. Hugo, the die-hard socialist, said that the whole point was to avoid detection by the oppressive bureaucracy. So the two of them chose to exile our family to a mountainous country where we had no friends and everyone spoke Catalan and Spanish. In the end, though, not much changed: my mother worked six days a week, making lots of money, while Hugo, whom my mother banished from the store regularly due to his uselessness, hung around our rented chalet in his ascot and knocked me around, harder and harder.

He'd smacked me in the face once or twice in Foix— stinging new ends to our daily arguments—but it wasn't until we got to Andorra that war was officially declared. One day after school, I provoked him about setting the table—my favorite way to make him angry was to remind him of his masculine chores—and he charged at me and hit me with such force, I was knocked backward. It was the closest that he'd come to giving me an out-and-out thrashing. Usually, he preferred a more subtle form of roughing me up: kicks, punches, and shoves delivered in an almost offhanded manner. This time, he meant to kick my ass. I remember being almost impressed, thinking, *That hurt. Wow, he's strong for such a little guy!*

Later, when my mother saw the giant bruise forming on my face, she flew into a rage that surprised Hugo and me both.

"Don't you ever touch my son again, you hear me?" she told him, practically snarling. "I am in charge of the discipline in this house. Hit him again and you're out."

Hugo lowered his head and apologized. After that, he was careful to hit me where it didn't show.

And so when he handed me a box of chocolates after I'd

already had my after-school snack, I was suspicious. Mon Chéri chocolates? "And your mother made you *daube de bouef* for dinner with *millefeuille* for dessert." I didn't need the sixth sense that my grandmother always told me I had to know that something very bad had happened.

At dinner, my mother abruptly excused herself from the table, leaving Hugo to serve dessert. Later, I heard her crying in her room.

My mother's crying went on for another day, alongside Hugo's smiles and special treatment. He even drove me down the mountain to the bus stop instead of making me walk through the snow like he usually did. When my mother was finally able to compose herself, she and Hugo asked me to sit on the couch and said that they had something to tell me.

"Eric," she said, unable to make eye contact, "we have sad news. Your father was climbing a mountain, La Rhûne. He got tired and told his friends to finish without him. By the time they got back down, he'd had a heart attack."

I felt my breath catch. "A heart attack?" I said. "Will he be okay?"

My mother began to cry.

"No, Eric," she said. "Your father is dead."

Hugo rubbed her back and offered me more chocolate.

I knocked the box from his hand and ran to my room. My father could not be dead. It simply was not possible. He lived far away and I did not see him often, but the fragile web of my existence depended on knowing that he was out there and that he loved me, and that someday, when I was older, we would travel together and hike mountains all over the world, as he promised me. The tears came quickly then as I realized that my mother would never lie about a thing like this.

There was a lot of shooting in the TV shows and movies that I watched after school with Hugo and I often wondered, what did it feel like to be shot? When my father died, I stopped wondering. Metal tearing through flesh sounded like a walk in the park compared to the hurt I was feeling.

I cried on my bed for hours and when it felt like I had shed every tear I had, I pulled out the box of letters my father had sent me since the divorce and read through them all, skipping the parts where he told me how mad he was at me for not writing him back (not my strong point) and how I should learn to behave and be more respectful of Maman and Hugo. Instead I focused on the lines telling me that he loved me and missed me, and where he described all the fun we'd have on my next visit: we'd go see the fishermen, he'd let me count the money with the prettiest teller at the bank, and we could go to any restaurant I wanted so we wouldn't have to eat Francine's food. He'd teach me to play trumpet like Louis. I replayed all of the conversations we had, the times we played in his house, our picnics in the countryside.

In the morning, I finally came out of my room.

"Should I pack, Maman?" I asked. "I mean, for the funeral?"

"It already happened," she said. "You're only eleven, Eric. You should have happy memories of your father alive with you, not of some body in a coffin."

I could not believe it. Did she want me to kill myself? How could she have kept me from my father's funeral? My sadness turned to rage and then the anger to numbness. It was like my heart had been cooked in a bonfire. There was nothing left but ashes, but the ashes still hid a few lethal flames.

· · ·

My father had died, but I missed only one day of classes. I decided I'd rather go back to school than spend another day home with Hugo. It was a snowy day and as usual, I walked from our house to the place where I waited each day for the school bus that would take me down the mountain. Sometimes the snow would come down so hard, the only thing that let me know the bus was coming was the two red lights in the distance. I sat down on the ground, at the base of the mountain, and I spoke, out loud, to my father.

"Papa, if you are really dead, give me a sign," I asked.

I saw two red lights and I thought it was the school bus, but then a dozen more lights appeared and they circled my head like a red halo. The lights went around and around, whizzing just above my head, for what felt like a very long time. I had asked for a sign, and I received it. When the school bus finally pulled up and the door opened, it took all the strength I had to leave my perch on the mountain.

Goodbye, Papa, I thought, as the bus ambled away. *Goodbye. I love you. I'll love you always.* I love you still.

10

:::

Chez Jacques

As much as I learned to love food by eating in my mother's and grandmother's kitchens, Jacques was my first introduction to a real chef. After I had my first meal at his restaurant, I began heading straight there after school to watch him cook. Why would I spend my afternoons doing homework or getting picked on by Hugo when I could hang out with Jacques? I never offered to help, and he never asked; I was only allowed on the kitchen side of the counter when he wanted me to taste things. Jacques had kids, a son and a daughter my age, but I don't think they were interested in the restaurant. But by the time we met, food—shopping for it, making it, eating it—was my greatest happiness, and Jacques could tell this from the moment we met.

It soon became clear to me that even though he put on a show, Jacques wasn't actually crazy or cruel. He just played the part of the town character. Everyone in our tiny capital knew that the native Parisian was a career parachutist who'd fought with, and cooked for, the colonial troops of the French army in the Vietnam War. What he had done in the war—what he might be capable of when vexed—was anybody's guess. By keeping his knives sharp and his temper sharper, Jacques kept people off guard—which is how he liked them.

In the kitchen, Jacques was a master of the classics, but his travels as a soldier meant his menu included dishes that you rarely saw on restaurant menus at the time: Vietnamese spring rolls, lacquered duck with five-spice, and *poulet au bambou*. These dishes not only made him justifiably celebrated, they also added to his outsider reputation.

Jacques used to say his mother-in-law was his true teacher in the kitchen, not because she taught him to cook but because she educated his palate. According to Jacques, during the year that he lived with his wife's family, menus were never repeated unless favorite dishes were requested. Mercedes's mother did everything herself: duck confit, smoked magret, foie gras, preserves of all types, sausages, marmalade.

He spoke lovingly about going out to jazz clubs and returning late at night to his mother-in-law's cold tomato *tortilla* waiting on the dining room table for him to enjoy. After she passed away, no one ever dared to make that tomato *tortilla* again, not even him.

If it wasn't for Mercedes, his wife, Jacques said his family might have starved: the personification of the phrase *"a casa del herrero, cuchillo de palo"*—in the blacksmith's house, they use sticks for knives. He was so busy with the restaurant that at home he never prepared anything more complicated than

Brie and bread. But Mercedes made the most delicious paella in the world, *tortillas* that looked like two-tiered cakes, stuffed calamari, cannoli, and garlic chicken. Mercedes was especially gifted at cooking fish with *sofrito*. And she never wrote a recipe down.

Jacques said that because of his life in the military, he had traveled the world. In every place, he made friends. In every place, he had girlfriends. He might have stayed in another country if not for the wars that brought him to those shores in the first place. But he and Mercedes made a good pair. He had grown up in Paris in a neighborhood of European immigrants: Polish families and Gypsies, Spaniards and Italians. To him, Mercedes and her large extended family felt like home.

"Only if you cook what you love and truly understand will people be happy with your food. Running a restaurant is not a popularity contest. It is not really any way to get rich. But you can make beautiful food and you can live your life your way," he told me one day as he was writing out the menu on the chalkboard. *"C'est toi qui décides.* It must be you who decides."

One afternoon, while I was polishing off a steak *au poivre vert* at the counter (the important thing, Jacques instructed me, was to get the pan as hot as you could before adding the meat—that, and always give good wine to your butcher), an English couple walked in and told Jacques they'd heard about him. He was in a good mood and he winked at me to let me know he planned to have a little fun with them.

They knew about the set menu and asked what he was making for dinner.

Jacques smiled and said, "Tonight it's spring rolls, *poulet au bambou,* and *baba au rhum.*"

The couple understood what spring rolls were, but asked him to explain the *poolay, sill voo play.*

"*Alors,*" he said, his round face widening with a wicked grin. "*Je vous explique. C'est le poulet*"—he started clucking madly, his arms flapping crazily—"*avec le bambou.*" He made wild stabbing gestures as he ran toward them, screaming.

Believe it or not, they stayed.

For Jacques, it was imperative that he choose which customers had the privilege of dining in the restaurant. For him, inviting guests into his restaurant was more intimate than inviting them into his own home.

The more I came to watch Jacques cook, the more he began to share his recipes with me. Eventually, Jacques even taught me the secret to his perfectly crispy *nems,* or Vietnamese spring rolls, which I had loved since one of my earliest visits. To start, he puréed onions and squeezed them in a towel to get out all the water. "That way they won't oxidize, so they won't taste like onion in your mouth. *Tu comprends?*" Then he mixed the onion with carrot, crab, ground pork, chopped vermicelli, *champignons noirs,* and a few eggs. "Are you watching, Eric? Mix it all together to make the farce. Use your hands. Then, when you put it in the wrapper, you have to be extra careful not to use too much farce, and not to roll it too tight."

My mother was happy to hear that he started frying them in a pan of cold oil, just like she did. She was less happy to hear that he let me eat twelve *nems,* versus her limit of eight at home.

I was fascinated by this new world of flavors and techniques that he had brought into the mountains; I imagined Jacques in the jungles of Vietnam, chopping down bamboo trees with a machete to make dinner for his regiment, or learning how to fold rice-paper wrappers from an old village woman. I began to imagine what other dishes lay beyond the borders of France, Spain, and Andorra. My mother introduced me to Moroccan dishes, and from my grandmother Maguy, I had enjoyed many great Italian dishes. My father's mother, Emilienne, taught me the tastes of Provence. She cooked with a lot of passion too. My grandmother Emilienne was shyer and not as expressive as Maguy, but I loved the time I spent in her kitchen. She cooked from her own garden and the radio blared opera—the bellowing tenors and cascading soprano voices that she loved.

The Asian influence was becoming big in France at this time, and Jacques played a big part in bringing those flavors to my life. So did my godmother, Rosemarie. She was an old friend of my mom's: a pretty strawberry-blond woman who never married and never had kids. On the occasional Saturday, Rosemarie would take me out to a Vietnamese restaurant and a movie. But I did not just eat Vietnamese food in restaurants. My mother also had friends in St. Tropez who were Vietnamese immigrants. They were the ones who taught my mother how to make Vietnamese spring rolls, and through them, that influence entered our kitchen.

Vietnamese cooking was very different from the Italian and Provençal influences, which were more prevalent during those times. In the early 1970s in France, mint and cilantro were not common in savory food. Mixing pork and shrimp was also unusual. Rice paper was a completely new ingredient in French cuisine, and the sweet-and-sour dishes that you find in

Vietnam, like pork caramel, were not common flavors for the French at all. As a kid who was obsessed with food I loved all of it: not just the spectrum and combination of flavors, but also the way the food was served; it felt entirely new to take a piece of chicken and dip it into an aromatic, like fish sauce, before each bite. And of course, to a kid, chopsticks were highly entertaining.

At his restaurant, Jacques showed me how he made his *mousse au chocolat* without cream—just dark chocolate melted with butter before adding an egg yolk and folding it all into meringue with the lightest touch. He made it in the same scratched glass bowl, using the same aluminum fork, for years.

Everything at Chez Jacques was cooked with love and care. Serving only a few dishes meant that he could spend all the time he needed to baby his food: he would take an entire morning just to make a *tarte tatin,* something I would never again see in a restaurant kitchen. On weekend mornings that I was there, he showed me how to first melt the butter and sugar in the skillet, and how to nestle half of the apples in the pan and cook it all very, very slowly, as though he had nothing else to do that day. It was my Saturday-morning cartoon.

But Jacques's *baba au rhum*—the rich, yeasty cake soaked in dark rum with just the right hint of vanilla—was my true addiction. One day I asked if his mother had taught him the recipe.

"No," he said, holding up the bag of supermarket flour. "The recipe's right on the package. But when you cook a dish with passion, you elevate even a box recipe."

He was the culinary king of Andorra. Jacques, my hero. No bullshit, no pretension, just quiet mastery that seemed to come from his bones, and a true love of cooking that you could see, feel, and, most important, taste. When he wasn't trying to scare people, he was making them truly happy.

Watching Jacques over the years, I came to understand how much hard work goes into being a chef. Each night, Jacques's dinner service was a one-man show with triumph after plated triumph. But the next morning, he always had to start over from scratch, no matter how tired or hungover he may have been. He told me that despite decades in the army, he'd never really known hard work until he opened a restaurant. He made every dish himself and never took shortcuts. There was no one to help him in the kitchen, not even a dishwasher. But Jacques was happy to go shopping all morning and then come back to his restaurant and cook all day, and at the end of the night, to scrub his own pots and pans. As much as he loved to create exquisite meals, I began to see that what Jacques loved most was the autonomy. And as I moved from middle school to high school, that mixture of great food and great independence started to appeal to me too. I began to wonder what it would be like to cook for myself and on my own terms.

Jacques had a pension from the army, so he didn't need to work so hard, but he had no choice; it was in him. When he saw someone swoon over his chicken marinated with ginger and star anise, served with all of its juices in a then unheard-of bowl of hollowed-out sourdough bread, it was worth more to him than the hefty price they'd paid for the privilege. He was happy to have clients and do his little act. It was his life. More than happy, he was content, and that contentment came from the fact that he was cooking the dishes he chose, for the customers he approved, in a restaurant that he owned. He was a free spirit and lived, in that way, totally independently. It was a contentment that I felt too, but only when I was around him. He never encouraged me to become a chef, only to eat whatever I wanted, but maybe that's because he could see that the desire was already in me. I couldn't see it at the time, but what began as a refuge from home and an escape from Hugo became my truest school.

⠿

11

Caviar Like Ice Cream

For all of her glamour, my mother loved being outdoors as much as I did. She needed the break. The boutique made our whole affluent lifestyle possible. The transparent coats, short skirts, and clingy sweaters made by Courrèges were incredibly popular, and my mom was the only person selling them in a petite boutique in a tiny country with no sales tax.

Come Friday night, every curve of Andorra's dangerous mountain roads was bumper-to-bumper with French and Spanish residents coming to buy clothes, liquor, cigarettes, perfume, and watches in the makeshift capital, where the traditional stone buildings with their slate roofs were being torn down to make way for a nondescript late-seventies boomtown. My mother's boutique was set off the main shopping street in an arcade called the Galerie de Paris. She had an eye for fashion and even I have to admit: no one wore those clothes better than my mother. Part of her success was that she was not just a great salesperson, she was also the embodiment of the brand, the way that Ralph Lauren came to symbolize a preppy lifestyle during the same era.

Come Saturday, her boutique was so crowded that she had to lock the door after every tenth customer. The line of women seeking the latest Courrèges styles stretched to the end of the arcade. People bought five or six of one item at a time; my mom had to restock before opening the door to the next round of customers. As her business got more and more successful, my mother began to groom employees she could rely on to watch the shop while she was away. Our weekend camping and hiking trips became a sacred refuge.

Outside of the time I spent with Jacques, the only true serenity I found was in the mountains. On Saturday mornings, we loaded our backpacks with tents, sleeping bags, and so much food and wine that Hugo's friend Roger often came along. Roger had owned a fish market in Toulouse, but had sold it by the time he and Hugo became friends. He was semi-retired at that point, and a good companion on the road. He made Hugo more mellow, helped my mom, and was funny and kind to me. Our weekend hiking trips were welcome escapes from the tension in our home. It was as if we could only be a family when we were on top of a mountain. Every time, I could feel my whole body relax as we disappeared up the foggy peaks for two days of hiking and eating, the men happily carrying backpacks of food and bottles of champagne and Bordeaux.

There are dozens of lakes in the mountains of Andorra. During our years living there, we'd gotten to know which waters had the most trout to be caught. (Hugo, of course, fished with fly larvae, which were banned.) My mother would poach the just-caught trout in a big pot set over a camping stove. When the fish was almost done, she would add a dash of vinegar to the *court bouillon* in which she was poaching the trout. That burst of acidity caused the skin of the fish to turn blue—a rare delicacy I'd read about in one of her cookbooks. Then she would reduce the liquid, emulsify it with a little butter, and serve it as a sauce for the fish.

Typically, we'd leave our Jeep on a sliver of gravel at the side of the twisting road and hike in for a few hours. Once we set up camp, we gathered the green flowering branches from wild rhododendron bushes (domestic rhododendron is poisonous, especially the American variety) to fuel our fires. I tried to name all the wildflowers with help from Roger, who was a local. Whenever we were thirsty, we drank the snowmelt from a lake or stream. We scrambled up the narrow trails between the rocks until we came to the next pass. We edged sideways along icy cliffs, using hooks to keep from slipping, and one time got stuck in place while a fog rolled in and blotted out the path. One of our favorite weekend excursions was to hike past three lakes, over a mountain, and into France.

The walks were always intense—try as I might, I could never pass Hugo, who motored ahead of us on his stubby legs. My determination to put him behind me always got me to the top. During the moments when I wasn't competing in my mind, the beauty of the endless mountains filled me with a sense of expansive calm that I began to crave. I started keeping a notebook listing each mountain and how long it took me to hike to the top. My legs and lungs were strong from walking up and down the mountain paths of Andorra. I was getting stronger every day.

After we'd reached our destination, we would make camp for the night. I had my own tent. Whenever we went camping in the snow (somehow it seemed like a perfectly normal family activity to sleep outside in below-freezing temperatures), our dog, Yuki, slept next to me to warm the tent with his breath. At night I read my favorite book by flashlight: a *Reader's Digest* volume on New York City, filled with pictures of all the famous buildings and people. As much as I loved my outdoor life, for some reason I was determined to live in New York. My quest to get there became a climb of a different kind of mountain.

Often, in the spring, we'd have my favorite meal: a salad of white *pissenlit,* or dandelion greens, picked wild from beneath a patch of melting snow. (The dandelions were baby-white because they hadn't yet seen the sun. Later in the spring, they would turn a brilliant verdant green. But in early spring, they are still white, tender, and sweet.) My mother would toss them in a mustardy vinaigrette and serve them with lamb chops grilled on a piece of slate—a typical Andorran preparation in which the charred meat takes on a slight mineral spice. Finally, she'd prepare a fricassee of chanterelles that we'd gathered while hiking in the woods on our way to where we would set up camp.

During these meals, I imagined my father next to me, telling me what a strong hiker I was and planning our next climb. I always talked to my father when I found myself in a dangerous spot, imagining what it must have been like for him to die on the side of a mountain. His words of wisdom, which came to me as flashes of good ideas, always got me to safety.

· · ·

Madame Amparo was the town psychic. She lived in Spain but like so many, she came to Andorra to do her shopping. She was a blond fifty-something woman, dressed in a simple but chic dress and, in the winter months, a vintage fur coat. Madame was gifted and when she came to Andorra, there was no shortage of people who wanted to book time with her and hear her predictions. More than just a psychic, Madame Amparo, many of our friends and neighbors believed, had the power to heal, and they often requested that she visit their loved ones in the hospital, where it was said that she could cure even the most devastating illness with her warm touch and powerful prayers. Her work was rooted in the New Age, but the benefits were so well proven that no one questioned the validity of her gifts. She was as well-regarded as an acupuncturist might be today.

There were only fifty thousand residents in all of Andorra, which meant that everyone either knew each other or knew of each other. Because my mother's boutique was so successful, everyone knew her, and they also knew that she was on her second marriage and that she had one son and a young daughter.

So when Madame Amparo approached me in my mother's boutique one day, I knew who she was and didn't rush away from her. On the contrary: I had been using the Ouija board for years and had a great interest in the spirit world and questions of spirituality. After my father's death, I began to use a glass and board to call to the spirits. My little sister, Marika, was my unwitting accomplice, but I was determined to get as many messages as I could from the other side, so I made her move the glass with me, even though she didn't know what we were doing and often laughed, thinking it was a game.

"Eric Ripert," Madame Amparo said, using my full name, as she always did. "I have a vision for you."

I hoped that the vision involved food and a girlfriend because I was hungry and longing for love.

"You have a bright and powerful aura, Eric Ripert," she said, closing her eyes and tracing the air above my head with her small, wrinkled hands. "You will live in a city surrounded by water."

I liked the sound of that—New York, after all, was surrounded by water. Once, when I was in the sixth grade, I took my piggy bank to the travel agency in town to see how much it would cost to fly to New York and spend a weekend at the Waldorf Astoria. They were kind enough not to laugh at me and just encouraged me to keep saving, explaining that I had quite a long way to go.

"You're going to work in a famous restaurant right by the water," she continued. "Tall building, very luxurious . . ."

Madame Amparo handed me a necklace with a cross on it, a cross of Caravaca, which she implored me to wear around my neck. "The original cross of Caravaca was found in Spain in the fourteenth century," she explained. "It contained a fragment of the very same cross upon which Jesus was crucified. But even a copy of the cross can be potent. This one has the full power of protection because it has been blessed by a priest."

She said that the amulet she had given me, a double cross with two angels, would protect me from violence as long as I wore it. I put the cross on immediately and almost never took it off. I wear it to this day.

I think that somehow Madame Amparo sensed that the

violence that would be of greatest danger to me came from within: my short temper, my anger at the injustices that I saw around me, and the rage that had already begun to build inside of me. Or maybe knowing that I was without a father or brothers, she intuited that I had a longing for protection and gave me a symbol to remind me that spiritual protection was always at hand.

If you asked me at age fifteen what I owned, I would've told you nothing but the clothes my mother still bought for me, my hiking boots, a few books, my skis, and my beloved BMX motorbike. It would take time for me to see that my mother had given me a gift by bringing me to Andorra. Growing up in a small town, with a mother whose business was central to the city, meant that I was surrounded by characters like Jacques and Madame Amparo. They knew me, and what's more, they watched out for me, and dreamed for me of a life beyond the mountain range. Ask me now what I own and I can tell you with confidence that among my richest possessions are the memories I have of the people of Andorra, people like Madame Amparo, who made our village not just a place between France and Spain, but also a bridge between the stark reality of my present and the rich possibility of my future.

That fall, I entered the ninth grade and the time came to decide what educational track to follow. The principal called me into his office and said, "You're not performing well as a student, Eric. We have to find a solution."

Thinking of Jacques and my love of hiking, I told him that I wanted to be a chef or a forest ranger. I was in love with the mountains, but even I knew that I'd never pass the tests on biology, botany, and the like. On the other hand, I knew that I loved to eat. I loved the experience of fine restaurants, and the great chefs of the day were my rock stars. I had a book from the library on the best chefs in France and studied it every night before bed, to the point that I dreamed about Paul Bocuse, Michel Guérard, and Georges Blanc. I'd never been allowed into a kitchen, but I'd been watching from the doorway my whole life. If I learned to cook, maybe I would be able to repay all the people who'd given me such happiness at the table.

After several more conversations, we decided that I would try to get into a top cooking school. The principal spoke to my mother and told her that he had a friend at the hotel school in Perpignan, and he would see what he could do.

Jacques was hacking up lamb for a curry when I told him my decision. He stopped, cleaver in midair, and beamed at me for a second before catching himself.

"They'd better watch out," he said. "You're going to eat all the goddamn dessert."

I remember that afternoon well because a little while later, André, one of Jacques's suppliers, came by with a selection of caviar for him to taste. André, I learned, had also served in the French Legion, and he and Jacques went back and forth with stories about their bravery and the feats of heroism they had undertaken to save the honor of Mother France.

I had eaten at fine restaurants since I was a little kid, but I'd never tasted the tiny black pearls André took from a large jar in an insulated bag. It was a two-kilo tin, almost five pounds of top-notch beluga caviar.

Jacques handed me a spoon—not a tiny mother-of-pearl caviar spoon, but a big soup spoon. Then he dug in, taking a huge scoop of caviar and popping it into his mouth.

I had seen Jacques eat and drink dozens of times by that point. But his reaction to that caviar was quite unlike anything I'd ever witnessed. He was in heaven. I stood with my spoon, unsure how a jar of fish eggs could elicit such a gratified response.

Jacques gestured for me to dig into the caviar, and still unsure, I politely scooped out a small amount. He took the spoon away from me and scooped out a heaping serving. I swallowed it and was surprised at how the flavor filled not only my mouth, but also my nose. I loved it—the saltiness, the richness, and the briny finish as I swallowed it.

"Do you like it?" Jacques asked.

"I love it!"

"Then don't be shy," Jacques said. "If you are to be a chef, these are things you must know. Eat more."

I grabbed another spoonful and closed my eyes. It reminded me of having sea urchins as a boy, at a seaside restaurant in Cannes with my father. He told me that "even if you eat a thousand sea urchins, no two will ever taste the same." I thought the same must be true of caviar: the flavor was that rich, that strange, that complex.

André explained that caviar is one of the world's oldest delicacies. "It predates the invention of champagne and was enjoyed hundreds of years before oysters."

Jacques took another scoop of caviar and winked at André.

"My wife better watch out tonight," Jacques said.

I must have looked puzzled—I had no idea what he meant.

"Caviar," André said, diplomatically, "is a very good mood enhancer. It is used, among the wealthy, to cure depression."

The memory of trying a food for the first time imprints itself into the flavor. A happy memory can make a food delectable, make you crave it, savor it, and, when it is gone, dream about the next time you will have it. Every time I have caviar, I am a teenage boy in Andorra, hanging out with my friend Jacques, eating spoonful after spoonful of beluga, downing it like ice cream.

12

::::
::::

A Waiter or a Cook?

That September, I found myself at Le Lycée du Moulin à Vent, and I was back again in Perpignan, where I had attended boarding school. It was a well-respected institution where fifteen-year-old boys came to learn how to cook and run hotels, and an even greater number of teenage girls came to learn how to become nurses, beauticians, and hair stylists. I wasn't thrilled to be sharing a dorm with fifty other boys, but somehow I managed to avoid the *bizutage*—the violent hazing that was a rite of passage for most first-year students. The older boys kept a slight distance, seemingly fascinated by my exotic Andorran background and designer clothes. Being different became an advantage. While the other first-year students were constantly getting their beds upended in the middle of the night, or having water splashed on their faces while they tried to sleep, I was left alone. (Theft was also part of the freshman welcome, but again, not for me.)

At that time, vocational school wasn't a training ground for the great chefs of France. Most of my classmates were guys who just wanted to get a comfortable job with good vacation time at a school cafeteria. A position at a nice hotel was about as high as they aimed. There were more than a few borderline juvenile delinquents in our midst. Instead of sending them to a correctional facility, the courts shipped the boys they thought could be saved to Perpignan for the rigid discipline. As we would soon learn, the "brigade system" was as military as it sounded.

You'd think my mother would have been upset by this blue-collar path—the equivalent of training to be a plumber or electrician. But for her, chefs were men like Bocuse, and restaurants were temples to good taste, rivaled only by her dining room. I wasn't apprenticing a trade; I was on my way to becoming a chef and cooking fine food. I saw it the same way. Sure, I would have loved to become a forest ranger. At fifteen, I thought that all a ranger did was spend his happy days hiking and daydreaming. But in my heart, I wanted to dedicate my-self to becoming a renowned chef—no matter where I had to start. The year was 1980. There was no such thing as MTV, much less the Food Network. My goal wasn't to become a ce-lebrity chef, but rather to cook in the best kitchens, creating the most refined food, in the kind of places that my mother read about, the kind of restaurants where one planned a reser-vation for months in advance because the meal was as valuable as a vacation, a one-of-a-kind journey of textures and tastes.

I made some friends, but when I wasn't studying, I was infinitely more interested in spending my time off with the beauty-school girls. The only problem was, I was too shy to talk to any of them. However, because they outnumbered us, the girls weren't shy at all. They approached me in gangs in the cafeteria and between classes, teasing me about my green eyes and saying they could tell I was a good kisser. Unfortunately, I was too lame to do more than take them to dinner or a movie. Then what? While the guys around me managed to smoothly talk the girls into their beds, I finished school with all the same awkwardness around girls with which I'd started.

The first-year curriculum was basic but thorough: knife skills, sautéing, braising, grilling, broiling, baking, plating and decorating, breaking down animals, filleting, preparing master sauces . . . Escoffier 101, as laid out by our classic course book, le Gringoire et Saulnier.

Our teacher, Monsieur Chaput, was a hapless guy who'd lived in Andorra, but with whom I felt no bond. He tried hard, but struggled to teach us because he wasn't a very good cook and wasn't very confident in his own mastery of the techniques. Maybe it was for the best that he wasn't very rigorous. Standing on my feet for six hours after spending the morning in classes on management, history, foreign language, and so forth was challenge enough. We were expected to commit recipes and skills to memory after just one demonstration, and it was up to me to make it work.

It was in culinary school that I learned the difference between cooking and eating. Prior to my second stint in Perpignan, I was a fine diner and as I saw it, food was art. At vocational school, I was being taught how to cook, but I was frustrated by how basic the dishes were. I was like a kid who had grown up listening to Chopin, then showed up at music school, never having actually played an instrument. I mean, when you listen to Chopin all the time, you want to become Chopin. And then you go to music school and all you're doing is plunking out *do . . . re . . . mi* for hours at a time. It's boring as hell, and not why you enrolled. I was impatient to create great meals and not so excited about starting with the basics. Why were we spending hours learning how to hold a knife or mince a shallot when we could be making nouvelle cuisine? True, I didn't know how to cut a chicken in eight pieces or make a béchamel. But in the two- and three-star restaurants I had been to, they were *way* over the béchamel. Still, there I was, in school, making the most basic of dishes—*salade Niçoise,* potato-leek soup, an omelette.

A typical cooking class went something like this: While we slumped in our chairs, Monsieur Chaput would stand at the blackboard and explain the day's dish, beginning with the technique. Let's say it was *navarin printanier,* a lamb stew with spring vegetables. He'd say, "This is a braise. We braise the meat because the meat is tough and therefore we have to tenderize it. So we cook it for a long time and we make a stew with it. Here are the techniques to make a stew: You sear the meat in a hot pan; the oil has to be smoking. Then you're going to flip the meat when it's caramelized—don't move it until it's sticking to the bottom of the pan. That's where you get the flavor. Then you're going to remove the meat from the pan. Then you're going to add the brunoise of onion that you've cut and the clove of garlic and the bouquet garni." And he would explain how to make the bouquet garni and how to cut the onion and so on. Still with me?

After we'd changed into our whites, we'd go to the kitchen—a big room divided into stainless-steel work areas—

where we'd cook individually, in groups, or in pairs. We'd look at our *bon d'économat,* a list of ingredients, and get what we needed from the refrigerator. For the stew, we'd start with the lamb. For that dish, we might be separated into groups of four guys standing around a standard-size cutting board, taking turns chopping a couple pounds of lamb into cubes, and yet it still took forever.

Once everyone had finished, Monsieur Chaput would say, "Okay, we'll slice the carrot first, because otherwise the cutting board will smell like onion." You learn how to do a dozen cuts in culinary school and when you see the photos in your textbook, they seem simple enough. They include some you might even use in your own kitchen: large dice, *bâtonnet* (which are, as they sound, like small batons), medium dice, *allumette* (think matchstick French fries), small dice, *brunoise* (very small dice), and *fine brunoise* (super-small dice). But you have to learn how to do these cuts with a variety of ingredients, and they all respond to the knife differently: celery cuts differently than leek; cutting an apple is not the same as cutting a carrot. If the vegetable is too soft, then a *fine brunoise* is a nightmare; it becomes like mush on your cutting board, just a horrible baby-food-like texture. And accuracy is important. At home, no one is measuring your matchstick fries. In even a one-star restaurant, an *allumette* has to be ¼ inch by ¼ inch by 2½ inches, and any sous-chef worth his salt will be able to tell at a glance if you've screwed it up.

Then there is the question of speed. Back in culinary school, it would take my classmates and me ten minutes to dice half a dozen onions. First we had to remember the knife grip that we'd been taught, repositioning our hands a hundred times. Then we had to painstakingly practice the proper onion dice: even slices lengthwise across a halved onion just up to (but not through) the stem end, flipping it on its side and repeating the exact same way, then laying it flat again and running the knife perpendicular to the other cuts. It was boring, but at the same time I was conscious that I needed to master the knife skills that I didn't have. If I wanted to be the best in the class, I was going to have to stay ultrafocused, studying twice as hard and practicing on my own time and weekends when I was home until the movements became second nature. I needed to keep going through the entire process, exactly like learning piano scales. Even Chopin didn't start with a sonata.

Instinct in the kitchen is something you develop very, very slowly. At sixteen years old, my passion for cutting onions was just not there. Today when I cut an onion, I have fun. It's like a musician warming up by playing a simple song or piano scales. I love the craft and the contact, the sensuality of it. But at school, I cut so poorly that my hand was riddled with blisters. Eventually the joint at my index finger would become so damaged that my finger is permanently bent, ever so slightly. I was in pain and crying because of the damn onion. I didn't really *feel* anything about cooking. The onion was not talking to me! And ultimately, nothing we made at culinary school was as good as the versions I had eaten before, from Jacques, my mom, or my grandmas, Emilienne and Maguy; or at the Michelin-starred restaurants we would make pilgrimages to.

I was ambitious, sure, but I was also totally clueless. I hated to take the guts out of a chicken and didn't understand why I had to waste time putting my fingers up the cold carcass, touching weird, slimy things. Cleaning fish was even worse.

When I protested, Monsieur Chaput just shook his head.

"This is something that you have to know how to do as a chef," he told me. "It's not optional."

"When I become a chef," I said, "I'm not going to take the guts out of the chicken. My cooks will do it."

"Maybe. But until then, you're going to take them out yourself." He plunked the bird onto my cutting board and that was that.

I stared at the bird and remembered all the times I had seen Jacques cook *poulet au bambou*. I had never watched him clean the chicken, but that didn't mean he didn't do it. For the first time, it occurred to me that though I'd witnessed my friend working very, very hard, Jacques had done much of the scullery work of cooking while I was still at school.

Learning how to make a perfect consommé was magical to me. When I was done, the broth was as clear and delicate as water, but it was incredibly tasty. It was my first experience of the importance of craftsmanship. I learned that everything had to be just right: cutting the vegetables just so; simmering the meat with the mirepoix and egg whites for well over an hour; keeping the liquid boiling at the right temperature so that the raft absorbed the impurities—too fast or slow and the consommé would remain cloudy.

Three months into school, I prepared one of my first truly successful soufflés, having first spent days slogging through lessons on how to make a Mornay sauce (béchamel with cheese and egg yolk, and a tiny bit of grated nutmeg). First I beat the egg whites until they were foamy and almost hard to the touch. Then I carefully folded the egg whites with the Mornay. When you make a soufflé, I learned, the mold, or baking dish, has to be very clean. And this is the trick: you paint the mold with softened butter, using upward vertical strokes because the butter painting upward will encourage the soufflé to rise. Then you dust the mold with flour. You have to make sure that the flour sticks cleanly and evenly to the butter, which is also essential if you want the soufflé to rise. Every tiny detail in that dish is very important, and I learned something about myself in the process. I loved the technical aspects of cooking: I loved the way that you had to master chemistry and craftsmanship, heat and timing, to make a dish like a soufflé come out well.

Restaurants love to serve soufflés because the timing shows off the expertise of the kitchen. The soufflé rises and rises. When it reaches its peak, it has a perfect browned color on top—and a soufflé will stay at its peak for all of about thirty seconds. It's a race against the clock to time it perfectly: from the oven to the client's table as fast as you can.

There's a way to cheat with soufflé. You can put in a lot of egg whites but less Mornay. The soufflé will stay high longer, but it won't have the same flavor. As much as I have an appreciation for the aesthetics of a dish, for me flavor was—and still is—everything. I had no interest in cheating.

When I went home for Christmas, I was feeling pretty bold. I wanted to impress my mother with what I'd learned. So I borrowed her Bocuse cookbook, found the recipe for the legendary foie gras soup that he'd served to President Valéry Giscard d'Estaing, and rode my motorbike into town to shop. The next night, we were all amazed that I had made my own puff pastry, molded it around the tops of the soup bowls filled with consommé, foie gras, and truffles, and baked it into golden

richness. My mother—the most refined eater I knew—
couldn't stop telling me how delicious it was. Even Hugo told
me he was impressed. Seeing it as a rite of passage, they let me
have wine for the first time. By my third glass I was so giddy, I
didn't make it to the cheese course. I just went straight to bed.

That year we were also trained in the dining room, the idea
being that in May the teachers would decide if we'd return to
study as cooks or waiters. Two days a week, we had to set up
and serve at the school restaurant, where locals paid ten dollars for a meal cooked and served by students. In addition,
we learned the basics of oenology, table setting (why the fork
goes on the left and the knife on the right), how to design
an efficient dining room, the use of the waiters' station, and
so on.

I liked being a waiter. I loved the formality of it, and the
way my actions and appearance could help create a mood. You
could say it's what my mother had inadvertently trained me
for. And I was good at it: having spent so much time in restaurants, it was definitely easier to relate to my experiences as a
client than as a cook.

As a kid, I bristled when my mother took me to task about
discipline. In my mother's house, even when we were doing
something as simple as packing a picnic for a hike, everything
had to be perfect: every dish had to be wrapped just so, every
napkin had to be folded, glasses had to be spotless before they
were packed even though we would be setting them down on
a patch of grass covered by an old blanket. In culinary school,
I learned what my mother had been trying to teach me all
along: there is comfort to be found in order. When you take

your time and do things properly—quickly, but without shortcuts—you have the ability to create truly great meals.

In part because of what I witnessed both in my mother's house and at Jacques's restaurant, I took naturally to the non-negotiable, army-like rules of the brigade system. Under the brigade, the chef is the command leader, and each cook has his station and short list of duties that he has to execute on command with perfect efficiency and consistency. Anyone who steps out of line is immediately—and sometimes brutally—reprimanded in front of the team.

On the one or two weekends a month that I went home to Andorra, I spent all of my travel time plus all of my noneating/nonhiking hours on my bed, studying my recipes from culinary school.

I also made time to see Jacques. Each visit, his influence on my decision to pursue cooking became clearer. He was so proud of me. Even more amazing was that he began treating me almost like a peer. I could tell he enjoyed having a fellow cook with whom he could talk about his passion, professional to professional, and I was happy to show off my growing muscles. Although I was barely a cook, I would swagger and act like a chef.

"So last week I made a *canard a l'orange*," I'd say, trying to sound casual.

"*C'est formidable!* How'd you do it?" he'd ask, pulling up a stool. I'd explain the method I'd learned and he'd tell me how he made his, making sure that I knew he was impressed.

It was up to the teachers, however, to decide if I would continue my studies as a waiter or as a cook.

In many countries, waiting tables is a working-class trade, or something you do just to pay the rent while you pursue a more creative profession. But in France, being a waiter is a proud vocation with a noble history. Accordingly, the dining room instructors were just as passionate about their work as the chef instructors were about theirs. So becoming a waiter began to look very appealing to some of the guys, especially when they found the rapid-fire pace of the kitchen both exhausting and perplexing.

No single person inspired more people to become waiters at the Perpignan culinary institute than the tough but fair manager-instructor of the school's restaurant, Monsieur Moccan. He was like a Dickens character: well into his forties, he was a chubby, slightly hunchbacked, bespectacled figure who strode through the dining room greeting customers with a voice that oozed charm and chastising staff with an entirely different tone that he used quietly, but severely.

Monsieur Moccan thought I was the best waiter in my class, and he took every opportunity to tell me so. He tried to push me, more than anyone, into a front-of-the-house career. But I never wavered. I wanted to work in the kitchen.

Toward the end of the school year, a decision had to be made about the focus of my second year, and consequently my career. Of course, my mind was made up, but I was only sixteen and the school was leaning toward placing me in the dining room. So it was decided that my mother and stepfather would make the drive from Andorra, have lunch in our restaurant, and meet the administrators to discuss my future.

To make the day as special as possible and afford me the opportunity to impress my family, Monsieur Moccan appointed me sommelier for the afternoon. The thought was that with nothing to do but pour wine and shuttle cocktails from the bar to the tables, an accomplished waiter like me would have an easy time of it and put a big smile on my mom's face.

I donned the waiter's uniform (white jacket with epaulettes, bow tie, black trousers, black socks, and leather shoes) and headed to the medium-sized dining room so that I could survey the hundred or so seats.

As the lunch service progressed and the dining room filled to capacity, a prestigious member of the French military came to our little academy. The colonel was accompanied by his wife and another civilian couple. I took their cocktail orders, got the drinks from the barman, and returned with one of our round, rimmed drink trays balanced on my open palm. Before I could get one glass on the table, something happened that had never happened before: I lost control of the tray, turning all four drinks over on the colonel and soaking his beautiful starched uniform. It was such a stupid error. With four glasses on the tray, I should have taken one from the front, but I grabbed one from the back. The tray was now unbalanced and before I knew it, it had toppled. To his credit, the colonel didn't lose his composure. He wasn't happy, but he was a true gentleman about my mistake and he sat there patiently while I patted his back dry.

Monsieur Moccan hurried over to the scene of the disaster and pulled me aside, supportive as ever. "Don't get stressed. The guy's going to be okay. He knows it's the restaurant of the school." At the same time, he wasn't going to let me run away from the problem either. "Go and fill up your tray again, come back, and serve them," he instructed. "You have to finish the job."

So I got the drinks again and came back as fast as I could. It turns out I came back too fast because they hadn't had a chance to clean the floor well. As I approached the colonel's wife, I slipped on the ice cubes from the first disaster and up-ended the tray on her. I expected her to start screaming, but I think they were all in shock at this point. Nobody said a word as I did my best to clean the table and help her dry herself off.

Once again, Monsieur Moccan whispered to me to gather myself, return to the bar, and finish the job. I remember thinking, *Finish? I was finished before I started.*

When I went back to the bar for what was now my third attempt to fill the same order, the barman could barely contain his laughter. But, with a sigh, he replenished my tray once again and I gingerly made my way back to my little table of horrors. I delivered three of the drinks without incident, then turned to the colonel. He nodded slightly to me. I nodded in return. And as I reached for his drink, the tray tipped, spilling a few drops of water—which I hadn't wiped off the tray—on his head.

That was it. The colonel shot up out of his chair and, in his commanding baritone, boomed, "That's enough! Get this person out of here!"

I flinched, taking a few nervous steps backward. But he wasn't yelling at me: he was yelling at Monsieur Moccan, who was suddenly nowhere to be found. Then I spotted him, through the little window of the kitchen door, laughing uncontrollably, unable to compose himself and return to the dining room.

"As for *you* . . ." the colonel shouted at me. And I stood there while he dressed me down in full view of the customers, who watched in awe, my mother slowly turning green, struggling to understand why the school so desperately wanted her son to become a waiter.

I never made it to my mother's table that day and I'm sure I didn't impress her, especially with where I ended up next: demoted to dishwasher. But at least I had found my way back to the kitchen. I never came out again.

13

Speed, Discipline, Stamina . . .
and Scrubbing Toilets

Luckily, the kind principal, M. Blaize, and the teachers who decided about internships recognized my ambition and secured me an internship at Le Sardinal, one of the most "gourmet" restaurants in the region. It also had the reputation of being run by the toughest chef. Two months there was supposed to test my determination, solidify my skills, and cure me of any prima donna–ish behavior—or so they told me later. Meanwhile, my less ambitious classmates were sent to cafeterias, chain-hotel restaurants, and tiny restaurants in tinier towns.

One of the teachers drove me an hour to the coast, winding through the seaside town of Collioure (known for its anchovies) and past the treacherously steep vineyards of Banyuls

until we reached Banyuls-sur-Mer. The seaside village was
made up of pink buildings with aqua shutters and terra-cotta
roofs, and a few tall, cream-colored apartment buildings whose
wrought-iron balconies looked onto the gray-pebbled inlet
and the flat sea beyond. Families walked along the short
boardwalk, stopping in waterside cafés. Compared to Perpignan, it was the Promenade des Anglais in Nice. Except I probably strolled that boardwalk only once that summer. I don't
think I even swam.

My teacher took me down an alleyway behind the main
street to show me to my room, informing me as we neared the
door that I would be sharing it with a waiter and another intern. I couldn't decide if the term "rathole" or "shithole" was a
better description of that hot, dank, windowless box, which
smelled like booze and night sweat. I threw my suitcase under
the camping cot that would be mine for the next two months
and followed my teacher to the restaurant.

Le Sardinal wasn't a two-star, or even a "Bib Gourmand."
It looked like a restaurant where vacationing couples came for
moules marinières when they could get a sitter at the hotel.
The long, narrow room had a nondescript bar on the left and
simple tables (at least they had tablecloths) on the right. There
was a piano set up near the kitchen entrance. It was beyond
basic. My teacher saw the disappointment on my face. "Don't
be a snob, Ripert. There are no dessert trolleys, but you're still
going to work harder than you've ever worked in your life."

The chef, who was about thirty, had a ruddy face and wild
eyes tinged with exhaustion. He sized me up without a word
and led me into the kitchen the size of a phone booth (of which
he took up about half), where four of us would be sharing
space. The signature dish of the restaurant was a classic an-

chovy preparation called *anchois à la crème de vieux vinaigre de Banyuls*. For the dish, the plate would be smeared with a mixture of aged Banyuls vinegar and crème fraîche. Then we'd top the mixture with twelve anchovies and serve it with toast. My job, I learned, would be preparing pounds and pounds of anchovies for the lunch rush. Next to my sliver of counter was a bucket containing about twelve kilos of anchovies packed in salt. Chef informed me that my job was to carefully remove the bones from each tiny fillet, then put the deboned anchovy into another jar filled with olive oil. By lunchtime, my hands had gone from tingling to numb.

Within the first hour of service, we'd sold more than forty plates of anchovies. I could barely keep up with the demand. It was a little stunning to see how hours of prep could evaporate within minutes, leaving you behind and in the weeds for the rest of service. Le Sardinal was apparently *the* spot, judging by the lines of people waiting in the plaza for a plastic table on the terrace. The chef was slamming out an impossible amount of food with his commis, a Perpignan intern-turned-employee (the other intern and I were only allowed to do prep work at first). From eleven o'clock on, there was no room for error—no room for anything—and the mood was incredibly tense. By two on my first afternoon, when the maître d', clearly drunk, told the chef to hurry up on an order, the chef simply picked up a stack of heavy serving platters from the pass and whacked him over the head. After just one blow, forehead muting the sound of the metal, the maître d' passed out.

The chef packed up his knives and left through the front door, the owner screaming after him.

Somehow, he'd returned by dinner.

Many times that summer at Le Sardinal, I felt like I'd been

hit in the head with a stack of platters. Six days a week, I worked from 8:30 in the morning until midnight. Most of my time was spent preparing the mise en place or peeling the eighty pounds of potatoes we'd need for fries, *pommes purée,* and duck fat–roasted *pommes sarladaises.* Then lunch service, then an hour off before dinner preparations began. The real battle started at night, as orders flew over the pass and the four of us worked back to back in furious silence to keep up. When it got too busy, the chef simply pushed us away so we didn't destroy everything. Even though I was more of a spectator in the whole process, the adrenaline in the kitchen was addictive; I was fascinated and terrorized and excited, and I wanted not only to survive but also to succeed. I wasn't learning haute cuisine, but I was learning speed, discipline, and, perhaps most important, stamina—things they hadn't taught us in school. My teacher was right: I'd never worked so hard in my life . . . or so I thought at the time.

When my mother visited, she was shocked by the restaurant's, shall we say, rustic charm. (The owner himself played saxophone during dinner, accompanied by a pianist.) She was even more upset by my living quarters and threatened to call the school to complain. "It smells like booze and vomit in here!" she said when she saw where I was sleeping. "What have you been doing?" I reassured her that it was my drunk roommate, who often threw up in his bed. Before she left, she gave me money and made me promise that on my rare days off, I'd go stay in the closest three-star hotel. Instead I used the money to take the chef to the hotel for drinks.

The chef was tough and relentlessly focused on the kitchen. At first I could tell he was pissed that the school had sent him a spoiled rich kid. But as the weeks went on, he saw my determination, one kilo of potatoes and anchovies at a time. Eventually, I was allowed to help with salads and desserts. As proud and grateful as I was, I still made stupid mistakes. Once, Chef dragged a box of twenty-five duck carcasses into the kitchen and told me to butcher them and freeze the breasts. With each magret, I slowly gained speed and dexterity. It took me about ten minutes per duck, which is a lot of time for a restaurant kitchen. Four hours later, I put the fifty breasts in one stack, loaded them into a giant freezer bag, and went home to take a quick nap before service.

Two days later, his head in the freezer, Chef screamed my name in a tone that made me fear for my life. He emerged holding a frozen tower of duck.

"Ripert, you bagged them all *together*?" he said. Everyone in the kitchen stopped and stared at me. Even the waiters came to watch. "How the hell am I supposed to pull one out and cook it? Didn't they teach you to wrap them individually? What kinds of morons are they turning out at that dump? Now get a knife and try to cut off three breasts without killing yourself."

My punishment that afternoon was to wash down the kitchen, including the dreaded salamander, which was used to broil dishes just before they went out. The thing was so crusted with heat-baked food and grease, I could have scrubbed until dawn just trying to remove the first layer of glazed-on muck. "Whatever you do," Chef said on his way out, "don't use water on it."

As soon as he was gone, I turned the high-pressure nozzle from the sink on it and had it shining in no time. So much for punishment.

When Chef came back for dinner, he nodded and pursed

his lips, impressed but clearly skeptical—there was no way I could have gotten it so clean without water. He reached up to turn on the switch and froze, stuck to the metal. His face turned white and his big body slumped to the floor. I'd electrocuted the son of a bitch. He looked up at me silently, too stunned to be angry. However hurt he was, I was sure I was dead. But he gradually roused himself and managed to make it through service in la-la land. The next day I learned a lot about scrubbing toilets.

By the time my two months were up, I had learned a year's worth of lessons. But that still left me a long way to go.

Luckily, my second-year teacher was a no-bullshit lifer named Monsieur Korbel, who had zero patience for mediocrity. Korbel had worked on *La France,* an ocean liner legendary for its cooks and waiters—many of whom had gone on to work at Le Pavillon in New York—and come up in the same generation as Jean-Jacques Rachou and André Soltner. In Korbel's world, Escoffier's haute cuisine was the ideal, and the chef had the power to demand absolute perfection from his brigade. He had no problem screaming at us or tossing a pan in the sink when one of us made a mistake—luckily the school wouldn't allow him to go any further. If we made a tomato salad that had a single seed in it, he literally threw it back at us and screamed, "I'm not a pig! I don't eat like that. Make it perfectly or go home." Then he'd grab a fresh tomato and a paring knife and, within seconds, transform the tomato into a lifelike rose, just to show us how precise you can be when you become a master of technique.

He was tough but good. We all knew that we had the best

teacher in the school, and we were happy to be pushed by him, competing to make an exact consommé or *vol au vent*. Finally, with each new dish, I was beginning to feel passion. Through conducting hours and hours of lessons and then standing over my shoulder in the kitchen, he taught me craftsmanship, discipline, and cleanliness: how to make the perfect *potage cultivateur*, a soup with dozens of pieces of diced vegetables, each of which has to be precisely cut; how not to talk, to stay in my station, to say, "Yes, Chef!"; how to keep my station and my person impeccably clean during service, and to execute all of his orders without questioning them. (Not talking was almost the hardest, right after remembering to clean my stove as I worked.) More important, he started to open up the instinct in me: I'd be working at the counter, and just by listening to what was going on in the pan on the stove behind me, I would know when it was time to add the onions or remove the meat. I was also learning timing—how, say, in ten minutes I'd have to be ready to send my *sole parisienne* to the pass. It was good experience, but it wasn't yet in my bones.

Outside of the classroom, a side of me that I didn't know I had also began to awaken. Both years, our dorm master was a young divinity student named Raymond Centène. He looked like an orthodox Johnny Cash—black clothes, long beard, very austere. But all the students loved him. This was a guy who would get up at six A.M. to drive me to the train station on a Saturday morning without expecting a thank-you. When he caught older students hazing freshmen, he brought swift justice to the dorm, which we accepted without question. He always had time to listen to our problems and talk about tough subjects. And despite his severe appearance and ultraconservative royalist ways, he was incredibly funny and warm. There was something pure and generous about him that we all responded—and, in my case, aspired—to.

As embarrassed as I was by my family's flashy lifestyle, I was entrenched in the material world of Andorra, where how many stores you owned and how big your house was determined whether or not you were a good man. Raymond looked into your heart and soul to find your goodness, and being around him made me realize that I had been looking at whether or not you had a Mercedes. Although I'd spent my childhood in a designer clothing boutique, my time in the mountains of Andorra had instilled a spirituality that I was only just beginning to sense; I had found a kind of religion in nature. Being around Raymond brought me to realize that it had been blocked by my extremely competitive, materialistic side, which at the time was more powerful than any spiritual ambition. His kindness and compassion made me feel that there was a better, more profound way to be in the world. I'd been looking at it all wrong.

I was always trying to run into Raymond in the dorm or the cafeteria, where we would have intense philosophical and religious conversations after I'd finished my homework. My mother was never religious, and even as a kid I was skeptical of my aunts' devotion. (My aunt Monique loved to tell the story of when, as a toddler, I refused to take communion with her at the cathedral in Nîmes until the day I saw the priest putting something in her mouth. Apparently I ran screaming up the aisle, "I want a cookie too!") I would challenge Raymond to explain—seriously—how Adam and Eve fell from the sky because she ate an apple. I mean, believing that, in the twentieth century? Good one, Catholics! He'd say patiently, "Oh, it's an allegory; it means X." He would try to rationalize the stories of the Bible and explain them to me in a different way, showing me that faith and intelligence could go hand in hand.

Not once did he try to convert me. He never had to tell me what I was doing wrong, either. All I had to do was listen to my own answers during our debates about, say, the value of money. He would ask me what was so important about being rich or famous (not that I was necessarily looking to be either, but I definitely didn't want to be poor), and obviously there's no smart way to defend the idea that you want to be rich versus spiritual and compassionate. I was shocked into silence by the emptiness of my answers. In that quiet way, he unlocked something in my heart and mind that made me question my values and my selfishness.

He also let us come up against our own faults (such as that selfishness) in other ways. Once he organized a weekend camping trip for a bunch of us on nearby Mont Canigou. The idea was to be together as a team, kind of like Boy Scouts. But I saw it as a way to show off. I told everyone how I had the best hiking boots and the best backpack, and what a great hiker I was. I was determined to be the first on top of the mountain. It was two hours before anyone else caught up to me. And then we realized that a slow kid had gotten lost in everyone's rush to keep up. Raymond was furious. My ambition had ruined his attempt to show us solidarity and teach us how to help one another. As he berated me, I became determined to be more compassionate and generous. To be more like him, at peace with his inner life rather than attached to the material crap surrounding it. At sixteen, the seed for aspiring to goodness was planted.

14

:::

La Tour d'Argent

In order to graduate at the end of two years, we had to be able to perfectly prepare two of the 120 dishes that we'd committed to memory. During the oral exam portion of the practice, we would be asked to recite instructions for a few of the dishes, from the list of ingredients to the step-by-step preparation. (I was asked to explain how to make pork curry, down to the correct measurement of salt and exact browning time for the one-inch cubes of meat.) Then we would go into the kitchen and each find a box of ingredients at our station.

"Ripert, do you know what dishes these ingredients are for?"

"Um, not yet?"

"You will make a goulash and a rice pilaf with *langoustine velouté*. You have three hours. Good luck."

The goulash. One of the dishes I was worried I wouldn't memorize correctly. I looked at my meat and vegetables, veal stock, and paprika, and got to work as calmly and methodically as I could. I cut the beef into neat cubes and sautéed it right away, because I knew I needed to get the braise going before I could do anything else. I began to hear M. Korbel's voice as I seared the meat on each side of the cube, taking care not to let it stick too much to the pan or get too dark, just enough to caramelize and create a flavor concentrate that would later be absorbed by the onions. Then I deglazed the pan with white wine, added my vegetable garnish, and let it cook. Meanwhile, teachers were coming around and taking notes over our shoulders, asking questions and murmuring a little bit of advice (in my case, don't forget the tomato paste). I could hear one of my classmates crying from the stress, but I stayed calm. In went the tomato paste with the onions and paprika. Finally, the *fond de veau,* or veal stock, was poured in and I left it to simmer. I could tell from the rich aroma that M. Korbel had taught me well. Now I had to *tourner* a basket of potatoes, giving each one seven neat, even faces so that they were identically carved into a shape something like an American football.

The rice pilaf was technically trickier: I packed the cooked rice into a *baba au rhum* mold and prayed that it wouldn't crack when I inverted it onto the platter. It did, but not so much that the creamy seafood sauce—made from roux and a fish fumet and mussel juice, then poured inside the ring— leaked out. While guys around me cursed their burned dishes, I decorated mine with bright red crayfish heads and quickly took it to the dining room before the rice dam broke. There, our teachers were joined by chefs from the region, who would judge our food based on taste, presentation, and technique. The ring, miraculously, held together, and I passed.

By the end of culinary school, I felt I was on my way to mastering the basics. I wasn't the best in my class—that was my friend Raymond Victor, one of the only students who had actual restaurant experience—but I had ambition.

As I climbed out of the Pont Marie métro station in Paris, I couldn't help but think of Madame Amparo, the psychic from Andorra, and her prediction for my future. I was on my way to my first day of work at the only three-star Michelin restaurant out of eighteen establishments that had responded to my résumé.

It was a rainy September morning and I was so excited that every sense was hyperalert: I can still see the pigeon gray of the Parisian sky, smell the exhaust from all of the cars and scooters, and hear them rushing past me. Rarely in my life have I felt so present.

As I followed my new map across the bridge linking the Île St.-Louis to the Left Bank, I fell into a trance, oblivious to the tourists brushing past me on their way to Notre-Dame. I was lured ahead by the strangely familiar limestone building rising at least six stories along the far bank of the Seine. Tourists were posing in front of the grand wrought-iron doors beneath an Art Nouveau glass canopy that seemed to float along the Quai de la Tournelle. The city's sounds fell away. All I could hear was Amparo's voice as she described the restaurant where I would work one day, in a city surrounded by water. I had hoped that her prediction would land me in New York, imagining all the skyscrapers there where a guy like me could learn the art and craft of being a chef. But when I stood in front of La Tour d'Argent and gazed up at its classic seventeenth-century façade, it felt like exactly where I was meant to be.

La Tour d'Argent was so old and so storied that it is even referenced in Proust's masterpiece, *Remembrance of Things Past:* "I have to return tomorrow to Paris to dine at the Tour d'Argent or at the Hotel Meurice. . . . M. Boutroux is to address us there about certain séances of spiritualism—pardon me, certain spirituous evocations which he has controlled."

I had been hired as a commis, or junior chef, and La Tour was celebrating its four-hundredth birthday when I arrived. There are pictures of me, dressed in medieval gear, wheeling out a giant cake at one of the many celebrations the restaurant hosted that year. But that would come later. I looked down at my leather briefcase, filled with the knives that my mother had given me for graduation from the Lycée du Moulin à Vent in Perpignan.

The letter told me to enter through the staff door, which was around the side. I climbed the grand oak spiral staircase six flights to the kitchen, where my stomach sank. The kitchen at my school was more modern, and five times as large. The doors to the garde manger refrigerator were wooden, bleached and pitted from a century of nightly scrubbing. The central stove, called a Waldorf, was a monster: fifteen feet of cast iron with a glowing red center that dared you to go near it. (The guy showing me around told me that I was lucky: a decade earlier, they'd still been using a charcoal-fed stove.) That beast made the kitchen hotter than St. Tropez in August.

When I entered the kitchen, twenty white toques rose from above steaming copper pots to show the damp, greenish-white faces of the cooks. They sneered at me as I discreetly dabbed away the sweat on my brow with the sleeve of my new leather jacket, which I thought made me look tough. Maybe not.

Even though they weren't that much older than me, these were men: fast and mean, muscular from real work, reeking of sweat and garlic. They'd been apprenticing in great kitchens since they were thirteen. By twenty, they were old masters. Me? I was seventeen, thin and wiry, with a culinary school education that didn't hold a candle to their years of training. A visible wave of excitement went through the room as the cooks picked up on a new scent, one that was even stronger than the aromas of melted butter, sautéing shallots, and that legendary roasting duck: fresh meat.

The sous-chef, Jean—a short, square, powerful man—told me to go downstairs and change, then come back up and wait for Maurice Guillouët, the chef poissonier, or head fish chef, who would be overseeing me on his station. Maurice arrived in his jeans and T-shirt, brushing away the wild hair that framed his gruffly handsome face. He was twenty-one—which at the time seemed so much older—and I immediately wanted to impress him. He had the kind of dangerous, rock-star charisma that comes from those who are truly good at what they do. That he arrived to work each day on a motorbike only added to his coolness in my eyes.

"Go mince some shallots while I change," Maurice said, jutting his chin toward his station before disappearing back down the staircase.

I ducked around as the other cooks were prepping for lunch service, reducing whole fish and vegetables into perfect portions with a precision and efficiency that would elude me for months. I found my spot at the end of the fish station. (And spot is the word: there were about six inches between myself and the next guy on either side.) I took one of my knives out of my suddenly ridiculous-seeming briefcase, grabbed a shallot with a trembling hand, and, before I'd even removed the skin, sliced open my finger.

I ran downstairs to the locker room. When I entered, Maurice was pulling on his pristine whites in the dingy changing area.

"Maurice? Hi! I'm sorry," I said, holding out my bloody finger. "Can you please help me find a Band-Aid?"

"You've got to be kidding. Where are you from again?"

"Andorra."

"Here," Maurice said, handing me a bandage.

We headed upstairs, the white paper toque I'd been given already sliding off my head.

When we got back to my station, I grabbed my knife, determined to prove that I could cook. Maurice took one look at me and his face fell.

"For Christ's sake. Do you even know how to use a knife?"

"Of course I do. I just graduated from culinary school."

That wasn't the smartest move. Back then, cooking was a blue-collar trade, like plumbing or bricklaying—not a prestigious career for boys whose parents took them to good restaurants. Real cooks—like the guys at La Tour—hated guys from culinary school. They believed that the only way to become a great chef was through apprenticeship and by surviving the physical and verbal abuse of the kitchen, not by memorizing recipes and taking notes and making a soufflé once a semester like I'd done for the last two years. Maurice laid into me, saying that I was a culinary-school baby. If I was going to cook three-star food for people, if I actually expected to produce dishes like *quenelles de brochet* and lobster bisque, I'd better learn how to hold a damn knife. Then he segued into a rant about how the chef must have searched high and low for the most unqualified commis in a special attempt to make his life hell.

Tirade over, he asked me to make the hollandaise, adding, as though it was nothing, "Thirty-two yolks, okay?"

"*Oui,* Chef," I dutifully replied.

This seemingly easy task would be the thing that broke me, showing me the gap between culinary school knowledge and real restaurant chops. To start, it took me almost twenty minutes to separate the eggs. None of the guys around me lifted their heads from their stations when I asked what to do with the whites. They were too deep in their tasks, moving with a smooth, mechanic urgency as they prepared their mise en place for the first service, slicing leeks as fine as eyelashes and "turning" carrots into perfect barrel shapes. Stopping for ten seconds to answer a basic question was unthinkable.

When I approached the Waldorf with my pan, the hairs on my forearms curled up and singed into nothing. I tried to ne-gotiate for my own twenty inches of space with a cook who was calmly adding lobsters to a massive pot of stock. But even then, I didn't have the strength to move thirty-two yolks and make a light and foamy sabayon. I didn't know to feel the tem-perature of the pan with the back of my hand. I didn't know how to instinctively intuit the right temperature to cook the eggs so that they would become that magical sauce. I didn't know and I couldn't ask—this was La Tour, not cooking school—so I failed, at the simplest of tasks. Maurice was so shocked when he discovered my incompetence that he said nothing, just took the pan out of my hand and looked upward, as if demanding celestial intervention.

Everything he asked me to do that first day was an echo of the hollandaise. I couldn't do it, I didn't know how. I wasn't able to help, when help is what a commis is there to do. Maurice was obviously running out of patience and struggled to come up with a task that I could actually handle. He sent me to get chervil and clean it for garnish—the most humiliating job in the kitchen, since it required no skill. Picking herbs was not where I should be starting. I turned toward the refrigerator and paused.

"What's chervil?" I asked. "Is that like parsley?" I mean, I'd heard of chervil, but I'd never seen it. Our school couldn't afford expensive herbs.

At this point, Maurice lost it.

"*Nom de dieu! Nom de dieu!*" he started screaming (the worst curse if you're Catholic), waving his arms in the air. "This is total bullshit! I'm going to talk to the chef." I'd totally killed the guy.

For a moment, everyone in the kitchen put down their knives and stared. Shocked and ashamed, I almost collapsed from the weight of the realization that everything I thought about myself was wrong. Maurice didn't think I knew how to cook. I was so stunned, I couldn't even say I was sorry. I just got my ass over to the refrigerator to find any herb I didn't recognize and prayed it was chervil.

I felt weak at work and the sense of vulnerability and panic only deepened when I was away from the all-consuming rush of the kitchen. On a weekend visit home to Andorra, I ran into Madame Amparo.

"You're having a tough time," she said, sympathetically.

No psychic ability was necessary to see that was true. I was pale from all my time in the kitchen and I had deep circles underneath my eyes, a very different picture from the tanned athletic kid I'd been when I'd left for my first big restaurant job.

"And you were mugged in Paris," she said.

This was also true; my mother had told her. But what she said next shocked me because it was something no one else in the world knew.

She peered at me knowingly and said, "You weren't wearing your cross of Caravaca. The chain broke and you left it on the nightstand to the right of your bed."

She was right. One night, coming home late from work, I was mugged in the metro. Two guys attacked me on an escalator. One guy held a knife to my neck and I was terrified that with the movement of the escalator, he might slip and slit my throat before I could hand over my watch and my wallet. The minute the men ran away, I reached up and instinctively touched my neck. I wasn't wearing the cross that Madame Amparo gave me. The chain had broken and it had been on my nightstand, just as she'd said. I had never doubted Madame Amparo's ability before, but now I knew for sure that she was the real deal. I'd gone out without the necklace she'd blessed for my protection and I was almost harmed. I vowed not to leave home without it again.

15

:::

Figure Eights

As much as Maurice hated working with me, Chef Bouchet made it clear that the situation wasn't going to change. "No matter what, he's staying. You're dealing with him," he was told. Before, Maurice had been manning the fish station by himself, sending out dishes for 120 covers a night. If he got rid of me, he'd be back on his own. But more important, no one said no to Dominique Bouchet.

At thirty-two, Chef Bouchet was young to be running the three-star kitchen at Paris's most storied restaurant. But he had the natural authority of someone twice his age. Handsome, powerful, and disciplined, he looked more like a movie star than a guy who'd spent a career behind the pots. Thirty years before the invention of Food Network and the popularity of celebrity chefs on TV, Bouchet glided through the kitchens of Paris like there was a camera following him. His every move was elegant and he executed complicated dishes with ease. At a time when the top chefs of the world were messy, slovenly characters with outsize personalities that said they didn't give a rip, like my friend Jacques, Bouchet was different. Even the way he put on his apron and toque was perfection, crisp and flawless. He was still a young man, but Bouchet had taken over one of Paris's oldest, most venerable restaurants. We were all in awe of him. He was the savior of La Tour d'Argent.

Bouchet had apprenticed with the great Burgundian chef Marcel Pouilly. And, like me, he'd attended culinary school. Paris at the time was buzzing with culinary talent. Among them, one chef stood out as the one to beat: Joël Robuchon. Bouchet and Robuchon had crisscrossed paths throughout their twenties at Paris's finest hotels and restaurants, always with Robuchon a little ahead of Bouchet. They had worked together at the opening of the Concorde Lafayette, with Robuchon as executive chef and Bouchet as one of his sous-chefs. Then Robuchon went to Hotel Nikko and Bouchet to Jamin. But when he was just thirty years old, Robuchon made a play and successfully purchased Jamin. He needed to discreetly get Bouchet out of the way, so he arranged for Jacques Sénéchal, the chef of La Tour d'Argent, to move to the Nikko. Robuchon then moved Bouchet to La Tour d'Argent and kept Jamin to himself. The rumor was that Robuchon was part of a secret society of Masons and that the extent of his power ranged much further than his stovetops. More than the rising prince of the culinary world, he was regarded almost as a mystic who could influence the rich and powerful at will.

With Bouchet safely ensconced at La Tour d'Argent, Robuchon hired a team of young, talented chefs, and set about reimagining the restaurant as an innovative showplace for an evolution of the increasingly popular "nouvelle cuisine." Within a little more than a year, Jamin was awarded an unheard-of two stars from the Michelin guide. Two stars were impossible for a small, newish restaurant in a city where many of the dining establishments had decades upon decades of experience. Robuchon became the talk of Paris. The restaurant had only a dozen tables and soon the waiting list was months long.

That was in the early 1980s, and the food world in Paris, which had so long prided itself on tradition, did not know what hit them. Having mastered the classics at such a young age, Robuchon became bored and curious, like a young Picasso playing with cubism. He reinvented the form of formal dining, stripping away the artifice of heavy sauces, and discarding old methods of cooking poultry and meat for hours at a time as if every meal should be as heavy as a Sunday roast. At Jamin, Robuchon quickly gained a reputation as a genius and a tyrant. There was no such thing as good enough in his kitchen, and you could taste the demands he placed on his staff in each and every plate. There were no dried herbs, only fresh. A sprig of parsley wasn't tossed raw onto a plate but rather flash fried, like tempura. Robuchon was the first chef in Paris to roast a rack of lamb in an herb-infused salt crust. He seared the lamb and then put it in a salt crust and cooked it very slowly. With this technique, you got the benefit of the meat both being seared and cooking very gently, absorbing herbs, flavor, and saltiness from the crust. It was presented in the dining room for show and then removed from the crust and served to the client.

Robuchon also reimagined the classic *île flottante,* or floating island. One part of the dessert is a meringue that floats in a *crème anglaise.* Robuchon baked the dessert in the oven in a mold and then studded the meringue with pink pralines. All of a sudden, a dish that had fallen off restaurant menus was reimagined as something new: visually beautiful and texturally different, with its almost crisp mold. In his twenties, Robuchon had won all of the major cooking competitions in France. These illustrious formal competitions were prestigious platforms where a chef could show off an elaborate, almost over-the-top formal aesthetic as well as a commanding mastery of technique. Robuchon had first amazed the food world at these contests, and he brought his drive to wow the judges and blast the competition to every dish he created at Jamin. His mashed potatoes remain perhaps his most famous dish, and they exemplify what his goal has been all along: to reinvent each ingredient and in the process transform something as humble as a potato into something almost noble.

From that aerie of culinary reworkings, Bouchet came to La Tour d'Argent. At La Tour, Bouchet was a hurricane of modernity, elevating and transforming the stale and stodgy menu into something exciting and new. His fights with the owner, Claude Terrail, were legendary: we knew it at the stoves, and the food critics knew it too. To survive, La Tour d'Argent needed to evolve. It was clear that Terrail thought merely hiring a younger chef would convince the media that the old place had been given new life, but Bouchet, trained by Robuchon, did not intend to be merely window dressing. He fought Terrail hard, and more often than not, he won. It was thanks to his modern vision that La Tour began to introduce lighter, nouveau dishes such as a warm poached scallop salad on top of mâche and monkfish, cooked *à la vapeur* with a *sauce vin blanc* on the bottom. At the same time, Bouchet peppered the menu with the classics that made Terrail happy, meals that patrons of La Tour had enjoyed for over a century—the pressed *canard au sang*, duck with green peppercorn sauce, the *quenelles de brochet* (pike) with *sauce mousseline:* hollandaise with whipped cream.

Bouchet's vision extended to the front of the house as well. La Tour was known for its arrogant tuxedoed waiters who had been serving there for decades and did as they pleased. Bouchet insisted that the waiters respect the system: no more sloppy behavior, walking *behind* the pass, the long metal shelf where dishes were plated and left for pickup.

I was incredibly lucky to have Bouchet on my side. One of his gifts was his ability to see the big picture. He assembled his team as if they were soccer players: you need the guy who can score the goals, but you also need guys who can pass, and young guys who can hustle. A good kitchen staff has to have a mix of skills and backgrounds, so that everyone is bringing something different to the table.

How did I end up at one of the crown jewels of the Paris restaurant scene when my knife skills were for shit? The answer, I would later learn, lay in Bouchet's ambition for change. He didn't need another line cook who had been trained to do things the old way. Bouchet was intrigued that I was from Andorra, another part of the world, with perhaps a different palate. He thought it was good for all those restaurant-trained blue-collar guys to mix it up with a culinary school grad. He liked that I came from a family where fine dining was part of our experience; as a young commis, this gave me an unusual perspective on the front of the house. But mostly I think he

could tell how motivated I was. I may have been just seventeen years old, but I was clean cut, obedient, and hardworking.
And hard work carried me through everything those first few
months because I was still learning how to be a cook.

The first week, it took me ten minutes to julienne a quarter-
cup of leeks. (It took the other cooks about forty-five seconds.)
I badly needed to improve, so during my lunch break, I'd hop
the métro two stops to my studio apartment on rue Broca and
practice cutting carrots in my own tiny kitchen. I knew that
once I came back in the afternoon, Maurice would be yelling
at me to speed up. I needed to have everything ready on time
for dinner—once service began, I'd get a sickening knot in my
stomach from the pressure; it took all of my strength to keep
my hands from shaking. As soon as the chef who ordered fire
started screaming over the microphone, yelling, "You fucker!
Where is that sole?" you could feel the entire kitchen tense up.
I would get so flustered, I couldn't hear a thing.

Two weeks in, I gave myself an opportunity to spend con-
siderably more time on my home knife-skills study. I was trying to lift a fifty-liter pot of boiling lobster stock for bisque—a
two-person job—and spilled it all over me. Rather than ask for
help with it, I had grabbed both handles and gone red in the
face as I tried to hoist the three-foot-tall pot. My muscles instantly stung from the strain: stomach, back, legs. I thought I
had a good grasp, but there was too much liquid inside. It
started to tilt and my hands were scalded by the bubbling
stock. In a moment of panic, I lost control. In school, they
trained us to immediately rip open our jacket and tear off our
pants if we got boiling liquid on ourselves. I stripped off my
checked pants, but I couldn't unlace my shoes in time. When
I finally peeled off my socks, layers of skin came off with them

as I huddled in the middle of the kitchen in my boxers and toque. My injury didn't stop the cooks from calling me out for my error—"Look at all that fucking lobster stock we have to redo, you waste of space!"—while Maurice and Jean wrapped my feet in kitchen towels and accompanied me to the doctor around the corner. The doctor informed me I'd be laid up for at least three weeks.

After a week in my top-floor studio, I was a little faster with the carrots—I was spending about two hours on them every afternoon. But I was miserable: embarrassed that I'd made such a huge mistake, anxious to get back and prove myself worthy of my job. So I showed up at the kitchen in blue Sebago boat shoes, which I was still unable to lace because my feet were so swollen and bloody, desperate to get back to work.

"Get the fuck out of this kitchen!" Jean screamed, although I could tell that he actually felt bad for me. Maurice took one look at me and sent me home for another ten days. It must have been like a vacation for him.

I was so bored, so homesick, it was almost unbearable. I had no friends or family, and I hated that damn Parisian weather. But I knew I was living my dream to work in a three-star restaurant, and failure was not an option. I was painfully aware that this was the chance of a lifetime. I had to learn, and learn quickly, no matter how much abuse I had to take. If I had to glue myself to the stove in order to stay there, I would do it. I went through hundreds of leeks and carrots, each one taking what seemed like an hour to finish.

When I needed a break, I would hobble over to the Pompidou Center and hang out in the plaza, watching the acrobats and guys doing tricks.

One morning, I found an old man doing tarot-card readings. He was no Madame Amparo, but I really believed in these things and needed whatever comfort or memory of home I could find.

"How much for a reading?" I asked.

I could see him sizing up the leather jacket and nice shoes that had been a present from my mother.

"Ten francs," he barked.

This was about two U.S. dollars at the time, and probably twice what he usually charged. But I was intrigued, so I opened my wallet and handed him the cash.

He gestured for me to sit on the dark green metal chair opposite him and then he shuffled the cards.

"Cut the deck," he ordered.

I did.

Then he laid out three cards. Each, he explained, would tell me something about my past, my present, or my future.

The card for my past was the Tower, which he said spoke of disaster, upheaval, and sudden changes.

"Are any of these true of your childhood?" he asked.

I shrugged. After all, wasn't the whole process of growing up one of change and upheaval?

When he flipped the center card, the one that he said embodied my present, it was an upside-down Three of Pentacles, which he said spoke to a lack of teamwork and poor work skills in my current occupation.

I was beginning to feel that the ten francs were well worth it.

"What about the future?" I asked, eagerly. "Am I going to be in Paris for a long time?"

"You see that card?" he said, gesturing at the Hanged Man. "You're stuck."

· · ·

Once I made it back into the kitchen, Maurice greeted me with grudging respect. It seemed like the bloody boat-shoe incident had made him finally understand how dedicated I was. Not that he made things any easier for me: the first thing he did was tell everyone the carrot-practice secret I'd revealed to him. And then he gave me twice as much work. But this time, I was up for it.

Within a few weeks, I'd figured out how to shell the langoustines (the secret: dislocate the first two sections of the body with your fingers and twist, then gently but firmly press on the tail while you pull out the meat). By the end of a month, I could finally handle the heat of the stove and had pretty much mastered the dreaded hollandaise. Watching Maurice make the sauce again and again (and listening to him yell at me again and again), I came to understand how to move the large pan on and off the heat—pulling it out, putting it back, pulling it out, putting it back—keeping a finger on its copper base to make sure that it was warm, never hot. I learned to make a continuous figure eight with my whisk to ensure that all sides of the pan were touched, rather than whisking in round circles as you might for a Chantilly. And I gained the fortitude to keep it up for the twenty minutes needed to get the yolks foamy, switching hands when the cramping got too painful. Sometimes the old guys would come by and make fun of me, watching my forearms burn.

Still, by mastering those thirty-two yolks, I had done something right. I was becoming a real cook.

16

:::

Garde

Paris is magical for tourists. But when you work in dark, almost windowless rooms until the middle of the night, the city is like a fairground after the carnival is shut down. I left for work in the dark, wet gray of the morning. And when I went home, it was after midnight. It was as if I'd just missed . . . well, everything. I could see the remnants of other people's fun—the cigarette butts, the empty wine bottles piled up in trash cans outside the cafés, the matchbooks with phone numbers scribbled on them that had been cast away—but by the time I arrived on the scene, the party had moved on.

At work, I was scared, confused, lost, lonely, desperate to prove myself—feelings that were only intensified by the rude bustle and gray demeanor of my new city. My mother and I became very close during my first two months at La Tour d'Argent. She would call me every day and encourage me to stick with it. "You can do it. You're good. You're strong." She wanted to motivate me and although I didn't always believe her words, the sound of her voice comforted me.

I missed the mountains and sun of Andorra, so I bought framed posters of nature scenes to hang all over my studio apartment. They didn't help much. But I had chosen my path, so each morning, before the sun rose, I made my way through the back door and up the stairs to the dark, smelly locker room at the top of five flights of stairs.

How does a chef make twenty cooks work in perfect synchronicity in a small, hot room, without sacrificing quality or speed? Every chef must find his way, but the historical kitchen brigade system is built on a universal truth: fear is a great motivator. At La Tour d'Argent, Jean, the sous-chef, did the intimidating so that Chef Bouchet did not have to. Bouchet spoke to Jean and Jean spoke to you. Jean was a terror, but everyone endured his outbursts and the way he beat us on the shoulders because he had such a good heart.

Though he didn't want to betray his soft side, Jean always knew exactly when to help you, and when to leave you alone. Because he saw Maurice and Chef Bouchet protecting me, he decided it was his job to help me build up the layers of toughness that are essential in the kitchen. Every time Jean looked at me, it was with a mixture of pity and professional consternation, like, *What the fuck are we going to do with this scrawny little kid?*

In the morning to say hello, he would start by whomping me across the back. "Eric Ripert! Badada! What new atrocity will you commit today?" He would hit me on the shoulder with all his strength whenever he walked by. I had to lock my knees in order to stay upright. Every night before I crawled into bed, I could see where bruises were turning from black and blue to yellow, and where new bruises were about to begin. Today this would be deemed unacceptable but back then it was not considered abuse, just part of life in the kitchen.

When Jean received the day's merchandise, the screaming began in earnest. The walk-in was on the lower level and he would shout, "Ripert! Move your ass! Go get your fish!" God forbid you put your mise en place in the wrong place in the walk-in. He would knock it over and then drag you down the stairs to clean it up.

The thing is that I liked Jean, and I knew he liked me too. He saw his job as twofold—to teach me the basics and make me less thin-skinned. He knew that both were essential to my survival in the kitchen. Any mistake I'd make, he'd say, "Ripert, you fucked it up. Tonight: garde!" Whack. Or "Lunch: garde!" Slap. It seemed like Jean used any excuse to trap me. "Do you know how to make a *beurre d'échalote*? Garde! Garde! Garde!"

Garde was when you had to stay after service to cook for the restaurant's owner, Claude Terrail, who ate around midnight, after everyone was gone. (He lived on the second floor, so the restaurant was truly his home.)

It was my responsibility to prepare Jean's mise en place as he cooked Monsieur Terrail's meal, usually a soup and salad. The soup was always freshly made, even if M. Terrail didn't always eat it. One evening a few months into my time at La Tour, he requested *poussin farci* with truffle and foie gras. If he requested an entrée, we usually sent out only half a fish or chicken. M. Terrail was known for having a small appetite and more often than not, we threw out the rest of the expensive dish. Once his entrée had been sent out, Jean left and I was stuck waiting for the boss to finish. The first dozen times I did garde, he never asked for the other half of his meal. It went right into the garbage. So one night, he had poussin. We would always send him one half of the poussin and the second half would be kept in the kitchen. That night, I was so tired and hungry and pissed off that I just grabbed it and ate the second half of the baby chicken.

Of course, that had to be the night when he requested the second half of his meal. It was nearly one A.M.; I was exhausted and hungry and, I was confident, soon to be jobless. I remember staring at the crispness of Monsieur's suit, wondering how the signature violet in his buttonhole was still fresh so late at night. After the captain came to the kitchen and asked me for the other half of his meal, there was a moment of silence as he took in the fact that there was truffle sauce dripping from the side of my mouth. I nearly threw up. The ensuing scandal almost cost me my job.

In those early days at the restaurant, I often made the kind of mistakes that I can imagine firing someone for today. Once when we went down to staff meal, I left twenty-four ducks in the oven. After they were burned to a crisp, they were just tinder for a huge gas fire. The kitchen filled with black smoke as the ducks burned and we quickly brandished fire extinguishers to put out the flames. Now at Le Bernardin, when a young chef makes what seems like a thoughtless mistake, I think of my younger self and remember, "I did things like that," and try to respond with compassion, with a tenderness toward the young cook I once was.

Jean whacked me at will, but he also regaled me with stories of his days as a young cook, when it wasn't uncommon to be beaten with cast-iron pans. "It was so violent then," he would say, as he shuddered, thinking about the chefs who would give you a black eye just for breaking a delicate *beurre blanc*. "It's so relaxed now!" he would say, visibly exhaling, as if the daily meal services were as pleasantly paced as a spin on a merry-go-round. I nodded as if I understood, but I couldn't imagine being any more scared or frantic than I already was.

All those nights I did garde, I didn't realize that what I was being given was a private opportunity to watch Jean cook. From my first day at La Tour until my last, Jean was always giving me the punishment of garde, garde, garde. I was so confident that he did it to screw with me that I didn't realize he was actually mentoring me.

Each garde came with a lesson, and although I didn't at first see it for the gift that it was, my brain greedily absorbed the information. Jean would say, "Let me tell you the story of the Belon oyster. . . ." And then he would proceed to give me a master's education in the belon: how it is one of the rarest oysters in the world, found only on the Riec-sur-Belon, a tiny sliver of culinary heaven in Brittany, located between the Aven and Belon rivers. He explained that the Belon oyster has a distinctly nutty taste, a result of the mingling of freshwater and salt water in that river. Then he would instruct me to taste, and to learn. It was the kind of leisurely lesson that could never happen in service, when plates are flying out the door at breakneck speed and there's hardly time to think or breathe, much less talk.

One night, I spent an hour sweating shallots while Jean watched, tasted, and then threw out my efforts.

"Again, Ripert! It's just a fucking shallot, are you an imbecile?"

I learned that every stage of cooking a shallot produces a different result.

"Taste it," Jean said. "It's too sweet. So what do you do?"

"Try again?"

"During service, you don't have the time, you have to fix it. Add a little lemon juice or jus from the vegetable stock." Then he handed me another shallot. "Try it again."

I peeled another shallot, chopped it, then put a little bit of butter in the pan. When the butter was nearly popping, I sautéed the shallot and quickly removed it from the pot.

When it cooled just a moment, Jean tasted it and made a face.

"You taste it," he said.

I did. It tasted bad but I didn't know what I'd done wrong—and I told him so.

"Should I add lemon juice, Chef?" I asked.

He whacked me on the shoulder.

"It's just a bad shallot. It will add a moldy, putrid taste to the dish. It can't be saved. But you should know that. Let's do it again."

As a seventeen-, eighteen-year-old kid, I didn't see that being assigned to garde was a rare moment of intimacy with the head of the kitchen. "Do you see what I'm doing now?" he'd ask as he stuffed the little bird. "You think it's painful to stay late? You feel that you are punished, and you are. You cannot know this, but when you are a commis, you want to be exposed to the maximum, because after that, you will never have the same exposure again. You should thank me." He was joking, but he was right. In the years to come, I would thank him again and again. *Merci,* Jean.

17

:::::

Hear Only What's Important

I bonded with the other young cooks in the kitchen because we were the suckers they roped in to things like getting dressed up in seventeenth-century clothing, complete with stockings, wigs, and brocade caps, and carrying a model of La Tour d'Argent made out of sugar around the restaurant to celebrate its four-hundredth birthday. The other commis showed me the secrets to setting up Maurice's station: put everything that we would need during the three hours of service close to the stove; make sure there was enough water in the couscoussier at the start of the night, because there was never time to refill it, and if the bottom burned, everything that we steamed in it would have an acrid, smoky flavor; keep the sauces covered and all the tasting spoons, ingredients, vegetables, and trays ready; put the fish on top of the tray and put it in the refrigerator; and so forth. What I hadn't learned in culinary school, and what the more experienced commis explained, was that my most important job was to give Maurice the tools he needed to perform, then stand next to him and help him finish what he'd started or give him whatever instruments he needed as quickly as possible. I was part Formula One pit crew, part surgeon's assistant.

Once service began, things got a little more intense. First I had to listen to what dishes were being yelled out, determine which ones needed to be made by our fish station, then remember them—in order. What needed to be done now, and what needed to be ready to serve in twenty minutes? The big problem was, half the time I didn't understand what the hell they were saying. I couldn't understand the vocabulary of the kitchen—what was that guy yelling over the microphone about threelangotwomardsfivepressedbillstwospudswithlotsofair?

In a busy restaurant kitchen, there are so many ways to get distracted. But Maurice had a gift for creating a bubble around himself: all that got into the bubble was the order that was being fired from the mic; all that survived in the bubble was exactly what he needed to prepare the dish.

Gradually, I learned to be ultrafocused like Maurice, to hear only what was important, organize the information, and stay calm enough to do the work—not easy when you're overwhelmed by a kitchen in action. If he heard "three *panachés de poisson,*" he would say, "Yes, Chef!" and forget about the screaming and just focus on those *panachés.* Maurice was also a master at staying ahead of the game, thinking about what he'd have to do next and getting me to reset the station to be ready for the next wave of orders. He somehow managed to keep an eye on the other stations as well, perfectly timing things so that his dover sole would be ready at the same time as Table 10's two racks of lamb *en persillade*. Of all the cooks in the kitchen, Maurice seemed to me the most disciplined, not to mention the most talented. It was almost like he didn't feel the pressure that the rest of us did.

In that kitchen, the highest compliment was silence. You either got screamed at or there was no feedback at all (which was good; it meant there was nothing to yell about). I learned this after two months, when the most incredible thing happened: I cut the carrot brunoise properly and quickly enough for Maurice. It was a complicated knife cut: first you julienne the vegetable, then you turn it a quarter and dice it. Each cube has to be exactly one millimeter all around, and you have to do it fast. There were days when I would brunoise half a dozen carrots, celery, leeks, and turnips. Each time I would take the tray to Maurice and he would say, "These are for shit. But they'll have to do." This was not that day. Instead, he did that rare thing in a kitchen: he praised me.

"Finally, you made it!" he said, slapping me on the shoulder. "It took you a long time, but you see? Whatever you thought was impossible, now you can do it. So you can learn more. You're ready." Notice that he didn't actually say I did a good job. But as I blanched the vegetables in salty boiling water and then dipped them again in ice water to stop the cooking and retain the vibrancy of the color, I knew that I had mastered something small but grand. The more the small things became second nature, the more I would be free, as a chef, to build on the foundations with even more complex combinations of tastes, textures, and colors.

Before long, I realized that each task was a lot like hiking in Andorra. There was only one way to go—up. All of those years of climbing mountains had given me an instinct for the ascent, a sense of how to pace myself, how to structure my approach—not through sprints to the top, but slowly and over time. Once I'd mastered the brunoise, I moved on to making a scrambled egg appetizer with crab on top. From there, I learned how to make a *sauce vin blanc,* and then a bisque. I remember the bisque was a big deal; Maurice was very proud of that achievement. Each of these dishes may sound very simple, but I spent a few months doing each of them poorly, then doing them acceptably, until I could prepare them with my eyes closed and know, with confidence, that they would be great.

I wanted to be as good as Maurice, so I emulated his every move. By his side, I learned not only focus and discipline, but also technique, speed, cleanliness, how to plate properly and fast, and the fundamentals of fish, of sauce, and of flavor itself. We were always tasting, tasting, tasting before service. He always had the right way to describe things so that I'd understand. As for the knife skills, to this day I can hear him yelling, "Not like that! Look at my hand! You put your fingers like this—that finger should be behind or you're going to cut it off!"

He constantly made fun of me, mimicking everything I said to Jean or Chef Bouchet in my thick accent and knocking my expensive clothes in the locker room. According to him, I would never learn to sharpen my knife properly, even though I did it exactly like everyone else. But Maurice's teasing was becoming more brotherly than humiliating. Whenever another cook made fun of me the same way, Maurice would tell them to fuck off and pick on their own commis, sometimes threatening them physically with his muscular body, built up from a lifetime of sailing and swimming in Brittany. Let's just say the teasing died down—or rather, it took place behind my back.

It was from Maurice that I first began to learn how foundational sauces were to the fine dining experience. In culinary school, I'd learned how to make a few of what chefs call "the mother sauces": the cold ones, like vinaigrette and mayonnaise, and the hot ones, like béchamel, velouté, and a brown sauce known in professional kitchens around the world as *demi-glace*. But few cooking schools have the budget to let a bunch of knucklehead would-be cooks experiment with the quality and range of ingredients that you use in a three-star restaurant like La Tour, which meant that I had a long way to go.

"*Nappé!*" Maurice shouted at me, holding up the spoon with sauce as thin as water running off the back of it. *Nappé* is a term that every young chef comes to hate, and then eventually to respect. When your sauce is ready, it coats the back of a spoon perfectly—a smooth liquid concoction of balanced flavors. *Napper* means "to coat" and sauces must have the right consistency in order to properly *napper* a dish.

I looked down, embarrassed. "I followed the recipe," I muttered. In a professional kitchen you work from memory, and obviously my memory had failed me.

"Forget the recipes!" Maurice growled. "You have to use your instinct when you are making sauces. What do your eyes tell you? What do you taste? Are you watching the clock and timing everything perfectly? That béarnaise sauce needs to be thick, like the consistency of a light mayonnaise. It should not run on the plate. And the color has to be bright, not 'tarnished' because it cooked too long. And you need to have a lift of sweetness—but you also need to have that sourness and richness."

As an eighteen-year-old kid, it seemed like such a tall order for a small pot of sauce: for it to be, all at once, bright and thick, sweet and sour and rich. And yet, as is true for almost anything, the more I practiced what Maurice told me, the better I became.

Sometimes when he had a few moments to spare, Maurice taught me things outside the purview of the fish station. It was from Maurice that I learned how to make a gastrique, a combination of caramelized sugar and a touch of vinegar. When added to a meat sauce, it gives the sauce more shine. A great gastrique can help rebalance the flavors in a sauce and help with the consistency. Maurice explained that a gastrique is a great back-pocket sauce, the kind of thing that separates great chefs from the more workaday hacks.

"Turn the flame down as low as it'll go," Maurice demonstrated. "Then let it reduce by half. Keep an eye on it so it doesn't burn."

I began to prepare a mushroom sauce while Maurice juggled three stocks: a crayfish stock, a fish stock, and a lobster stock for the famous lobster bisque.

I had cleaned and trimmed the mushrooms early in the morning, before Maurice came in. Then I heated the sauté pan with a mixture of canola oil and a generous chunk of butter. When the pan was hot, I cooked the mushrooms with a mixture of minced shallots, garlic, and thyme for just a few minutes.

Once the mushrooms were tender, I added a bay leaf and deglazed the pan with white wine. I reduced the white wine by half, then added some fumet, a concentrated, aromatic fish stock. I raised the heat, bringing the pan to a simmer, then reduced the liquid again. I had not known before Maurice's tutelage how much of cooking was chemistry, the use of heat to reduce and transform textures and flavors. I added the mushrooms to the sauce, which certainly looked thick enough, and let it sit in the hopes that it might thicken up just a little bit more.

A few minutes later, when Maurice stuck his spoon in the mushroom sauce, he held it up before he tasted it. The sauce perfectly coated the back of the spoon. Then he tasted it.

"Not bad, Ripert," he said. "But remember, in a sauce, you want to be able to taste all of the ingredients; one taste should never dominate. I am tasting more garlic than anything, you used too much."

I was crushed. "Should I do it again?"

Maurice shook his head. "Nah, I'm probably the only one who will notice."

At home, on my days off, I practiced making sauces. Even though I was in the fish station, at home I practiced more universal tasks, trying to learn the craft. Beef kidneys, for example, were not as expensive as ribeye, but required a great deal of technique to bring forth the flavors and make them delicious.

Upping my knife skills was important, but at the heart of it all was physical training. I needed to teach my hands to move so quickly that my brain did not have to tax itself in the execution of every chop and dice. Learning sauces gave me something more vital and more elusive: I began to develop, in the very smallest of ways, the instinct of a chef.

It seemed like it took forever, but every couple of weeks, I took a little leap in the kitchen. I mastered one cut, then got better at another. I learned the sauces of the fish station at La Tour and one by one, I was able to execute them with vibrancy and depth. The more that I was able to accomplish my tasks with precision, the more of a help I was to Maurice during service. Soon, whatever he needed, I was there to give it to him. Most of the time, we didn't even have to talk. And that's when he started to have respect for me; that's when he really started treating me like a little brother.

Maurice began to invite me out to have drinks with him and his friends after work. He found the fact that I was never able to score with a girl in a club endlessly entertaining. "You were slow dancing, you were both drunk . . . and nothing? Ripert! This is simply against the laws of physics! Do I have to teach you how to have sex too?" Maurice had a serious girlfriend, but most of the guys in the kitchen picked up girls at clubs or went to hookers in rue St. Denis, so the conversations were pretty raw—and nothing I could contribute to.

But then things got tougher on their own. About six months into my stay at La Tour, Maurice came to tell me that he'd been hired by Joël Robuchon to work at Jamin.

"Robuchon?" I gasped. "No shit!" All of the gossip in Paris was about the young chef, who had overseen a staff of eighty when he was just twenty-one. "How'd you do that?"

"Anything to get away from you," he said. "Finally, I'll be able to get my job done without having to answer stupid questions from a guy who can't even get laid in Paris."

I couldn't believe I was losing my protector in the kitchen, my big brother at the stove. But Robuchon . . . he deserved it. After Maurice left, the guys who had been afraid of him came after me, but at that point I didn't care. I was too focused. And too busy: as soon as Jean saw that you were comfortable in one station, he moved you to the next, where you basically started at zero.

I was quickly moved to entremets, which is preparing all of the vegetables and garnishes for the meat station. "Oh, God! I know nothing again!" I would cry when I went home. But then I'd work hard and figure it out. And as soon as I began to feel good about myself, they moved me again. Next it was garde manger, where I made all of the salads and cold appetizers—like truffle-studded duck terrine with toasted brioche or lobster terrines—as well as portioned the fish and passed it to the fish station.

After I'd been at La Tour d'Argent for eight months they tried to put me on the station that fried the *pommes soufflés*, but I refused. The translucent puffed orbs that accompanied the duck dishes were delicious and impressive, but incredibly hard to make. You were peeling, washing, and cutting potatoes all day long, and they often burst in the oil, splattering and burning you. To me, that station was the Siberia of the kitchen. There was nothing for me to learn. At that point, Jean and I had grown close enough that I wasn't afraid to speak my mind. So when I saw that he had put it on my schedule for the following week, I told him half-jokingly, "If you put me in that station, I'm quitting on the spot."

The crazy thing is that Jean listened. By then, I had imposed myself upon the kitchen through sheer resilience and hard work. No one could accuse me of being the spoiled kid with the nice leather jacket. Now I was the guy who could cut off a piece of my finger, bandage it, and finish the day.

So the next station was pastry. I didn't last long: I was

kicked off after I ate twenty-five strawberry tartlets and I don't know how many chocolates made for that night's petits-fours. After pastry came duck. Duck was the restaurant's specialty, whether it was served with green peppercorn or peach sauce, cooked *au sang,* flattened *à la presse,* or whatever they were doing. For four months, I was seasoning, roasting, and then spending hours breaking down about eighty ducks a day. I cooked so many that for years I had nightmares about those canards. Sometimes I was cooking and I burned all the ducks. Other times, I was being attacked by vicious killer canards. It makes me shudder to think of it, the amount of my dream time that was—and sometimes still is—taken over by nightmares about ducks.

I moved on to back sauce, where I learned more sauces and also made the staff meal every day, which required putting together menus of Escoffier classics that Jean had selected from the book, with appetizer, main course, and, twice a week, dessert. It was like cooking for my hotel school exam all over again. For my first dinner, I sautéed about a hundred trout for the entire staff, not just for the kitchen; I was cooking two or three trout in a pan and I had six pans in front of me. When you cook fish with the skins, the pan has to be very hot. I was in such a rush, I started with cold pans and then the worst happened—the skins stuck to the pan. I knew much better than to make such a simple mistake but I was already in the weeds. In my anxiety, I panicked. I just scraped the broken trout off the stove and instead of stopping to correct my mistake, I kept going, ruining pan after pan of trout.

I tried to cover my mistake by hastily arranging the broken pieces of trout on the torpedo-shaped platters. Jean was short and the platters sat on a shelf of warming trays above my stove.

When he walked by, I thought—I hoped, I prayed—*maybe he won't notice.*

But he did notice and what he did was jump up and slam the trays off of the shelf, sending them tumbling onto the floor on the other side. The whole kitchen stopped because of the commotion. Now the embarrassment that I felt at ruining the trout was compounded by the fact that the whole kitchen was privy to my humiliation. Jean glared at me and said, "I hope you have enough money to buy everyone sandwiches at the bakery." Then he stormed out.

Somehow I thought that because the trout was for a staff meal, he would let me get away with serving broken pieces of fish that had burned and stuck to the pan. But I learned that staff meal is not an assignment to be taken lightly: if you cannot cook well for yourself, how can you be trusted to cook well for the restaurant's clientele? More simply put, when all those trays came tumbling down, I got the message loud and clear: you don't give shitty food to the staff. And you have to learn your craft.

I was probably just nervous about that night. I'd finally met a beautiful girl and managed to ask her out. The younger guys from the restaurant would take me to the club La Palace, which was like a dating supermarket, to try to get me to meet someone. On my way to the bar I saw a gorgeous girl with long, dark hair. She looked at me and smiled, then started walking toward me. The next thing I knew, I was on the dance floor with this incredible beauty licking my ear. I felt like the chef at Le Sardinal when he turned on the salamander that I'd just hosed off. I could only imagine how she'd be in bed. We arranged to meet that Friday at the Trocadero at 7:30. I couldn't believe it: a date! Because she was traveling through

France, it was a onetime deal. Guaranteed, the cooks told me back at work.

And then the pastry chef announced that he'd gotten a table for four of us at Jamin on Friday. Robuchon! No one could get a reservation—not even with Maurice there. There was a three-month waiting list to try the restaurant that all of Paris was talking about. I was like, "Oh, man. Sorry. Can't do it. I have a date with that girl, remember? I can't just leave her standing at the Trocadero. I can't . . ."

"You have until five o'clock Friday to decide, Ripert," said the pastry chef.

In that hushed little dining room in the 16th arrondissement, I discovered just how finely detailed a dish can be. If I thought the food at La Tour d'Argent was three stars, Robuchon was on another planet. He served dishes that no one had seen before. A ravioli, the wrapper so thin it was practically translucent, was filled with langoustine and *nappéd* with foie gras sauce—a startling pairing at the time. We had a miniature crown of rice with rabbit, the rim of the plate painstakingly decorated with alternating dots of truffle, some so small we couldn't imagine how they'd gotten on the plate in time to be served. (The rumors that his cooks worked eighteen hours a day must have been true, I thought.) It was revolutionary compared to what I'd been learning.

I had dined at two- and three-stars like the Ritz and Taillevent with a few of the cooks (the owner of Taillevent was generous and so amused to see a table of pale teenagers in baggy suits that he paid for our meal when he found out where we worked) and had been blown away by the food and service.

When I dined at fine restaurants, I always appreciated the luxury, but I also admired the craftsmanship that went into creating the experience: the hand-painted plates, the hand-blown crystal, the true art of service. But Jamin was something else. This was genius. I now knew what direction I wanted my cooking to go in. Now I just had to get there.

During my year and a half at La Tour d'Argent, I was taught what a real kitchen is; I learned it in my bones. The brigade system is brutal, but it works. Without it there would only be chaos. Jean was tough but smart: he made us jump in to help anyone who was behind on his station, which meant that all of our skills stayed sharp and well-rounded. When I arrived, I had no idea how hard working in a kitchen would be. Psychologically, it was incredibly difficult: you're not supposed to cry, you're not supposed to say nice things, you can't wince when someone hits you. When I look back on it today, I think: *Wow, I am what I am because of that exposure to all those stations and all those shitty jobs* (though by the end, cleaning langoustines was actually fun—not that I let on). Because I made so many mistakes and burned so many things, I will always know what not to do. If a cook today tells me he ruined his hollandaise, I can tell him at exactly what step he went wrong, because I've ruined it in every possible way.

I thought I was pretty tough for a nineteen-year-old. And a good cook, too. I was ready for the next move. When Chef Bouchet heard that I was looking to leave, he called me into his office.

"I hear you've been looking for a job," he said. "You must understand one thing: I am the one who decides when you leave. Not you. And when you're ready, I'll send you to Robu-chon."

I was sure he was bullshitting in order to keep me there a little longer. But just a few months later, he called me into another closed-door meeting. "Ripert," he said, "Robuchon is looking for a good cook."

"And you're sending me?" I asked, half-joking, half over-whelmed with pride.

Little did I know I was being sent straight to hell.

18

:::::

Training Days

I n 1983, all of Paris was obsessed with Joël Robuchon. The thirty-eight-year-old chef was so famous, he was known simply as J. R. He had received the award for Meilleur Ouvrier de France when he was thirty-one, and then had gone out on his own to open Jamin when he was thirty-six. The restaurant earned one Michelin star just three months after opening, and a second star came a year later. The acquisition of even a single star can make the reputation of a restaurant. For a young chef to receive two stars in such short order was the equivalent of a young actor getting an Oscar for his second film. By the time I arrived at Jamin, Robuchon was more than a chef; he was becoming a legend.

For some reason, I wasn't nervous during the interview, which Chef Bouchet had arranged. I was more curious to meet this phenomenon and be in his kitchen, which didn't seem nearly as stressful as everyone made it out to be. We sat in his cramped, humble office at the end of the rectangular white-tiled kitchen.

As the staff prepared that afternoon's service, the room was as quiet as a museum gallery. I wondered if it was just made up, all the rumors about how intense it was to work at Jamin.

As he talked, I was struck by how gentle and modest Robuchon seemed. The brutality with which he was said to run his kitchen must have been an exaggeration. He was clearly driven, but he also seemed to live very much in his head. You had to talk to him for only a few minutes to see that he had an intuitive sense of the ingredients and a gift for innovation.

"Chef Bouchet tells me that you've come a long way in his kitchen," he said. I nodded, trying to disguise my happiness that Bouchet would say such a thing. "Do you think you still have something to learn?"

Was he kidding? For all I had learned at La Tour, there was so much I did not know. "I've developed speed and knife skills," I told him. "Now I need to tackle precision."

Robuchon seemed pleased with my answer. "Oh, I think you're in the right place."

I nodded again. I knew that I was in the right place.

He stood, smiling broadly, and shook my hand. "Can you start at the end of the month?"

As I walked out of the office, feeling both triumphant and nervous, I heard a familiar voice. "Oh, *mon dieu!*" It was Maurice, standing over a pot, simmering fish bones for stock. The pan was not as big as the stockpots I'd seen in other restaurants. This, I would later learn, was by design. Robuchon purposefully did not keep large pots on hand because he wanted to make sure that we made everything fresh. Pots came in two sizes at Jamin: small and medium. Even the cold storage area wasn't big, because he didn't want us to store much. "I thought I'd gotten rid of you. Are you following me, Ripert?"

Though they never lifted their heads, the cooks who worked shoulder to shoulder around him seemed to come to attention when he spoke. I remember thinking, *So he's the boss here too, even though he's still just the chef poissonier?*

I grinned back at him. "I'll see you in a few weeks, Maurice. You'd better be ready."

Maurice shook his head knowingly. "Kid, you have no idea."

Early on a Monday morning in December, just a few days after leaving La Tour d'Argent with the blessing of Jean and Bouchet (and a drunken farewell with the cooks), I was ready to start my new life. At six A.M. sharp, I spoke my name into the intercom behind a modern apartment building in the upscale 16th arrondissement. As if in a James Bond film, the heavy metal garage door slowly lifted and I stepped inside, going from one level of darkness to the next. It would be a full eighteen hours before I stepped out onto the street again.

My fellow cooks welcomed me into the locker room. They were pale and skinny like myself, and most were not much older than my nineteen years. I'd heard that most of them had already cooked in incredible places like La Maison Troisgros, a three-Michelin-star restaurant run by a legendary French family in Roanne. Several of the guys had trained with Alain

Chapel, one of the fathers of nouvelle cuisine who was internationally known for his *gateau de foies blond*, a delicate and near-impossible-to-re-create symphony of butter, heavy cream, and *foie de volaille*.

Even at the high end, Parisian kitchens tend to be small, making a métro car at rush hour look roomy. But even by those standards, the kitchen at Jamin was tiny. The station for garde manger, where I was starting, was behind the coffee machine and next to the dishwasher for the glasses. Even before service began, it was already loud, with hot waves of vapor bursting into the air as cooks helped themselves to espressos and wineglasses were given a second cleaning. Somehow, I was wedged into that tiny nook, along with an apprentice and the chef de partie. My responsibility in garde manger was to produce the salads and cold appetizers. As steam billowed all around me, I wondered how I would create dishes that were still cold when I sent them to the pass. *It will be okay*, I told myself. The kitchen seemed pretty relaxed, with much less screaming than I was used to. And besides, Robuchon was being so nice.

"He's like that for a couple of days," a cook whispered to me during my first staff meal. "But watch out: it'll change, you'll see."

I didn't believe him. Every restaurant kitchen has someone on staff who sees it as his job to convince you that the sky is falling. *He's just that guy*, I thought. I was sure that Robuchon was a quiet, humble genius. Even now, it's hard for me to believe that I was once that naïve.

By the middle of service, I was a little spooked by how quiet and focused the kitchen was. I almost missed the microphone at La Tour and the bellow of Jean swearing at us.

During a brief lull on my service, I saw that the fish station was in the weeds. Since I'd been cross-trained at La Tour by Jean and instructed to jump in and help those in need, I went over to Maurice and helped him at his station. Then I hopped back to mine. I could tell that Robuchon was impressed. He nodded at me and smiled, like I'd exceeded his expectations. But I hadn't done it to show off; it was just what I'd been taught.

Later, the sous-chef, Pierre Gosse, came over and leaned on my counter. "Congratulations," he said, his mouth tight. "Today you really scored some points with Chef. He apparently liked what you did."

One morning Robuchon showed me how to make a dish he'd "just thought up": *assiette belle de mer au homard,* a cold lobster salad. It was so complicated, I got dizzy as he went through it: The lobster has to be cooked just before service, he explained, because refrigeration killed the flavor of shellfish. The bouillon to cook the lobster calls for chopped carrot, onion, celery, a fennel bouquet garni, orange peel, star anise, and black pepper. You add a splash of sherry vinegar, but you have to be careful not to add it too soon or the acids in the vinegar will prevent the vegetables from cooking properly. Once the lobster has been cooked, you discard the bouillon.

The claws are cooked separately from the tail, for four minutes exactly. Then the tail is wrapped in plastic film and speared on a metal skewer—a little trick Robuchon had devised that kept the tails from curling up and allowed them to cook more evenly.

While the seafood rests, you prepare the dressing, taking care to whisk it constantly. The dressing calls for mustard, sherry vinegar, ground pepper, peanut oil, and truffle juice.

Stir in each element one at a time, then put the dressing aside. With a mini–melon baller, make balls of tomato, apple, and avocado, reserving the latter two in a bowl of lemon juice to prevent oxidation.

Then you have to decorate the plate. For the sauce decoration, you combine mayonnaise and tomato compote. For the cream sauce, you mix mayonnaise-infused mussel stock, crème fraîche, wine vinegar, and a drizzle of lemon juice. Beating the mayonnaise, stir in one ingredient after another: vinegar, crème fraîche, and lemon juice. Then reserve the sauce in the fridge.

Nothing was tossed in a Robuchon salad; everything was arranged as if in a still life. When it comes time to plate the dish, first you artfully brush the plate with the cream sauce. Then you arrange the pieces of lobster into a Y shape on top of the sauce, mimicking the shape of a whole lobster and its claws. Dip the small balls of tomato, apple, and avocado into the vinaigrette, and carefully arrange them around the lobster, alternating pieces of avocado, tomato, and apple. Sprinkle the lobster with chopped truffle, thinly sliced chives, and a few leaves of chervil.

Now you are ready for the dots. Dotting the plates with hundreds and hundreds of edible dots could drive even the most detail-oriented cook to the brink of insanity. The dots are a blend of delicately balanced sauces. The sauces were difficult enough to cook, but then to use them to decorate the plate with precision, battling the heat of the kitchen and the pressure of time, was, each day, a fresh slice of hell. Once the dots are finished, you complete the dish with a final turn of the pepper mill. Wipe the edges. One dish is ready to serve.

The hollandaise I made on my first day at La Tour suddenly seemed simple.

If you were to take out a pen and a piece of paper right now and try to make a circle of ninety perfect, evenly spaced dots—even if you are a good artist, even if you take your time—I could look at the paper and tell you where Robuchon would find fault. Imagine trying to do those dots with a sauce made of mayonnaise and tomato compote. The sauce is cold and thick when you start, but if you work too long, it warms up and thins. Sometimes, as I spent hours painting red dots around a plate, I couldn't tell if Robuchon was a genius or a madman. The answer, of course, was both.

Even the simplest dishes, such as a lobster salad, had as many as twenty steps. You could write the recipe down when you learned it, but during service, there was no time to refer back to notes. When Robuchon demonstrated a dish, you had to give him your fullest attention. *Watch with your eyes.* Listen to what he said. Visualize your hands moving the way his did. Eventually, after making a dish a hundred times, you got it.

Then it was my turn to duplicate the meal he had demonstrated. He pointed to the balls of tomato that I was trying to mimic. "I want the balls to be perfectly round," he said. "Perfect, perfect, perfect." Then he walked away. End of instruction.

That first week, he came over several times a day to correct my salad.

"Eric, don't do it like that," he'd say, taking the spoon from my hand. "You have to redo it like this."

If I did not rise to the occasion immediately, Robuchon would send support my way, often in the form of Pierre Gosse, whom I quickly learned to dread.

"Pierre, Eric didn't do a good job on that one," he'd say,

holding out one of my salads from the elevated platform where he stood, overlooking the chefs at their various stoves. "Go over there and show him how to do it." Pierre was quicker than we were and his plating more precise, but on a bad night—when Robuchon was in a mood and felt like we were all against him—even Pierre's version would be deemed lacking.

Incredulous, I asked myself, *How is it possible that the sous-chef of the most talented chef in Paris couldn't execute his boss's vision?* He had to have been a good cook. He'd worked with Robuchon at Concorde-Lafayette and Nikko. Perhaps he started out strong and somewhere, somehow, he fell off.

Looking around the kitchen, it suddenly clicked: everyone was so quiet because they were scared. There was no screaming, no plate-throwing, no bruising claps on the shoulder like I was accustomed to. The fear of not meeting Robuchon's demands was all it took to terrorize everyone into submission. Multiply that by the fierce desire we all had to cook to his standards and it was no wonder everyone was so tense. Almost immediately, I felt that pressure descend on me. It was like a guillotine had appeared out of nowhere, perfectly positioned above my head, waiting.

Within a few weeks, I was promoted to demi chef de partie (a step between commis and chef de partie) on garde manger, which meant that I was now responsible for all of the cold dishes: three salads and five first courses. I had an apprentice and a commis to help me, but even so, it was physically impossible to produce what was needed for twenty diners in the allotted time because each plate required so much attention to detail and precision.

Even Robuchon had to admit that sometimes what he asked us to do bordered on impossible. Once he came up with the idea to do red pepper lobster mousse with a gazpacho vinaigrette. We tried that dish for days but in the end, none of us could make it to satisfaction: the texture was hard to manipulate, and the combination with the lobster, while flavorful, was inconsistent. For a restaurant dish to succeed, it cannot be a one-time circus act. In a restaurant kitchen, you've got to be able to fire the cannon twenty times a night, five nights a week. Eventually Robuchon gave up and changed the lobster mousse to a tomato mousse, a dish that made it to the menu.

And then there were times when I failed simply because of inexperience: though I'd been trained well at La Tour, there was still much I didn't know. One evening during service, the chef poissonier asked me to open two dozen littleneck clams for him. A simple enough task, but I'd rarely done it before, and I was very clumsy. I was not a trained fish chef. I was still on garde manger: cold appetizers and salads. So I lined them up on the shelf and waited for them to open. When a clam opened a little, I shoved my oyster knife in and shucked it. When the chef poissonier returned, I handed him three clams.

"Where are the rest?" he asked.

I pointed to the shelf. "There, I'm waiting for them to open."

After a year and a half at La Tour, I had finally mastered the connection between thought and gesture—the ability to think, *I'm going to put this dot of sauce right here,* and to do it well. But Robuchon demanded a whole new level of precision.

Each plate was not only delicious, it was also a work of art, and it seemed to require some mysterious combination of magic and science to complete a dish and have it arrive at the diner's table looking the way it had just seconds before.

I had thought I was a strong cook, but at Jamin, I began to believe that I wasn't talented enough or seasoned enough to deliver Robuchon's vision. Once I sent my dish to the pass, I would shrink inside myself as I waited to hear his voice saying, "It's bad. Do it over."

If it was good, he said nothing. But during those long moments when you didn't know, when he stood, staring at your plate—and he inspected every dish—the not knowing made seconds feel like hours. If the dish was okay, he sighed heavily, as if, even then, he was being forced to compromise some element of his artistic vision. Then he would clean the rim, even if the plate was spotless. Then the plate would go.

But if, say, the baby shrimp in a salad didn't have the perfect petal-like *rosace* shape, each one curved like the petal of an intricately designed bloom, or if he noticed a speck of chive on a truffle, then he would scream, "Ripert, I'm not happy with you! This is not the way to do it!" He needed to let the whole kitchen know that you had not only erred, you had failed him and the reputation he had worked so hard to create.

Not even the smallest error escaped his attention, and I always feared that I was next on the chopping block. Only Maurice managed (mostly) to escape his ire—Maurice and the dishwashers. Robuchon was extremely gracious to the African men who worked as the dishwashers at Jamin. They never bore the brunt of his criticism, even when their errors were egregious. What concerned him was the customer, and as he could not cook forty-five meals a night by himself, it was us—

the cooks whom he trusted to execute his vision flawlessly, night after night—who felt the full force of his frustration. What happened away from the customer's plate and palate was of far less concern to him.

This leniency sometimes went too far: once Robuchon was giving a tour of the restaurant to a visiting Japanese dignitary between the lunch and dinner services. On that particular day, the dishwashers had decided to use their downtime to do their laundry. They hung a line from one end of the tiny room to another and after carefully cleaning their delicates, hung their socks and underwear to dry. Robuchon entered the kitchen, his face full of pride—until he looked up. Disbelieving, he ran up to the line of laundry, then slowly backed away from it. He tried to speak, but it took him a few moments to find the words. "What? What is this?" he sputtered. Then he turned to Pierre Gosse and whispered, "Please, take that down." He turned his guests around and took them out of the kitchen.

And yet, that afternoon, neither of the dishwashers lost his job. He seemed to understand that they simply didn't get it. He could, and often would, lose his mind over an ill-placed dot on a plate or a badly shaped tomato ball. But I had to give it to Robuchon. His focus was fully, and totally, on the food. Dirty laundry, even in the kitchen, didn't faze him.

19

∷

The Taste of Terror

At Jamin, every shift was a marathon. Each time that you lined up at the starting block, your fight-or-flight instincts were on fire and you wanted to say enough, I quit, I can't. Most of the time, when you saw someone break down on the line, the truth was that for them, it was over before the shift had even begun. If your sauces didn't come out right or you were behind preparing your mise or you overcooked an expensive ingredient, then you were screwed before the first diner even sat down and opened the menu.

I was on the train before sunrise every morning, rehearsing my morning prep in my mind. Each day I had only one goal: to execute my plates without Robuchon noticing me. As long as I didn't make some mistake that he caught, as long as my plate wasn't the one held at the pass for extra scrutiny—or worse, sent back to be done again—then it would be a good day. There were a hundred things to do before Robuchon came rolling into the restaurant at nine A.M. The earlier I arrived, the better chance I had of not screwing most of them up. When the subway stopped at Trocadero, the station nearest to Jamin, it was still dark. The only time I saw sunlight before work was at the height of summer, during the three or four weeks when my work schedule actually coincided with daylight. As I walked to the restaurant, I mentally went over the recipes that Robuchon had put on the menu for the season.

Robuchon did not believe in specials. He didn't believe in weekly menus. He believed that frequent menu changes meant that you sacrificed perfection for variety. If we were always cooking new dishes, he worried that we wouldn't have the luxury of executing them on the technical levels he demanded. So his menu was conceived by the season, and each recipe had more steps than any other I had ever encountered. It didn't help that the dishes were unlike anything that was served in other Paris restaurants. Every dish was a complicated pairing of ingredients that weren't usually served together: spiced sea bass with a verjus sauce; oyster medley with bay scallops and caviar. In culinary school, I had rolled my eyes at the humble dishes we were taught to make. Now I longed for something easy so that for once, I could pull it off without thinking. It was all so hard, there was no chance I would ever do it perfectly. No one who worked for Robuchon expected to shine. All you could do was keep your head down and try to survive.

Early in the morning I would at times almost forget to be afraid. But from the moment I heard the garage door open at nine, followed by his car driving in, the fear came rushing at me, a runaway car with no brakes. He walked into the kitchen noiselessly, like a ghost, but I always knew when he had entered the room. I didn't have to see him to know he was near. We could all sense him, the fear silently rippling through us.

The first thing he said when he strolled in was, "Come on, guys! You have to clean the kitchen!" If he was in a good mood, he would tap you on the shoulder and say hello. If not, he greeted you with a glare and chilling silence. You know how laughter can be contagious in a group? Anxiety was like that at Jamin, and I had caught it from Gosse and the other cooks.

The only reprieve in all the pressure was that Jamin, unlike most restaurants, was closed on Saturdays and Sundays. The catch was that our team worked double shifts Monday through Friday. We arrived around six, never later than seven A.M., and didn't leave until well after midnight. When Eric Gestel, whom we called Coco, came to work at Jamin, we all remembered his first day because he worked hard and was impressively capable from the beginning. Then around four o'clock, he took off his apron and asked, "When does the second team come in?" Maurice and I burst out laughing.

Maurice said, "You take a half-hour break and then you are the second team." Every day was sixteen to eighteen hours long, sometimes longer.

The grueling hours meant that we took shortcuts where we could. Everyone had his secret mise. On Monday we were required to start from zero, but that was absolutely impossible. So Friday night, we'd hide things just before we left for the weekend. I would tuck stupid, meaningless mise en place under the lettuces, like a mayonnaise or a vinaigrette base. The guy at the sauce station would stuff the chickens with things for his mise. Everyone except Maurice: only he was able to deliver things as quickly as Robuchon wanted them. The rest of us had to find tricks in order to be as precise as was demanded.

But we did the best that we could because we understood the pressures that fell on him. Robuchon had the challenge of running a tiny restaurant that couldn't possibly have made money: there were twenty-five cooks for forty covers (versus twenty cooks for a hundred twenty covers at La Tour d'Argent), and he bought the most expensive produce in Paris. We didn't want to waste or ruin any of the ingredients. We understood that he wanted everything done *à la minute* to preserve their essence.

In my mind, the only way I could give the chef what he wanted was to be "creative." It started with the rabbit terrine. He demanded that it be made fresh every morning and ready to serve by noon, but when made to his specifications, it would take at least six hours and eat up 75 percent of my attention— and even then there was no guarantee it would be up to his standards. To make the terrine I had to braise the rabbit and vegetables separately, then cut them into a perfect brunoise. The gelée had to be made using calves' feet to set it—never gelatin—and it couldn't be too firm. (All of these components were prepared in different stations, so I was always in someone's way.) The terrine needed to be built stage by stage, layer by layer, so that it would set while remaining perfectly soft, and the layers would almost float, one on top of another, sticking together instead of sinking. The challenge was to create volume and space in the architecture of the dish while balancing the elements of heat, the organic nature of the ingredients, in other words, how they might separate and change in just a few minutes or even moments of being left out of the fridge. We had to be good, but we also had to be fast. So there was that too—the constant, unending need for speed in a restaurant kitchen.

Often, the terrine wouldn't take in the short time allowed. It was so fragile that I had to slice it with an electric knife, rescuing the rubbery cubes of shiitake that popped out and painstakingly trying to fit them back in like a surgeon. I used dill to frame the terrine, almost like a painting. Once the terrine was done, you spooned gazpacho sauce around the base so that it created a perfect red circle around the dish. The trouble with the gazpacho was that tomatoes start to release water after a few minutes, breaking with the olive oil in the sauce, so again, you had to move quickly. Finally, I had to do those damn green dots. When the dish was executed properly, it looked like a perfect mosaic—for just a few minutes. Robuchon would take his time looking at it on the pass, my life flashing before me.

"Ripert! It's too hard."

"Ripert! It's too soft!"

"Ripert! Your vegetables are no good."

"Ripert!"

And that was only one of seven equally complicated dishes on my station. If he decided at lunchtime that I needed to make a new terrine, I wouldn't have been able to do it even if I had every cook in the kitchen helping out. So I decided there was only one way I was going to survive. I would make two or three at a time and hide them in my refrigerator, moving them to another fridge when he came to inspect my mise en place. This way I could just cut him a slice from terrine number two and pray that the fresh herbs hadn't turned brown.

"Ah, see? When you want, you can do it," he'd sometimes say.

This did not always work according to plan. "That terrine is no good! I don't want it!" he'd yell when he'd see a fleck of tarragon the same color as the gelée. "I don't want that terrine. Make it again."

It was one o'clock, and he had no choice but to use the terrine—even if I began a new one right then, it would never be ready for that night's service. Then he would settle for choosing just the right words to destroy me: "You really don't care about quality," he'd say. "I mean, seriously. How can you give me a product like that? What do you think you're trying to do? If you don't care—and clearly you don't—don't work here. Don't come back. Go do the kind of bullshit cooking you like somewhere else."

I knew that Robuchon had only become Robuchon by meting out the same punishing standards for himself. Picasso once said, "I am always doing that which I cannot do, in order that I may learn how to do it." I think Robuchon worked the same way. He wasn't merely challenging us with the nearly impossible as a test. Deep down inside, he needed to know just where the line was, how far he could push an ingredient, a technique, a flavor combination. I knew that every criticism he hurled at us, he had hurled at himself a hundred times. He was more than a simple perfectionist; he was a visionary whose goal was nothing less than to change the face of French cooking.

I'd worked at La Tour d'Argent; I knew that Robuchon's terrines and dots were to traditional French cuisine what Picasso's cubist paintings were to a roomful of Rembrandts. Moreover, his business model was one of those complex mathematical problems that only a supercomputer could solve: you take the most expensive ingredients and multiply that by X dishes, then divide that by Y, the infinitesimally small number of tables we served each night, then subtract rent, lightbulbs, linen, and tableware, as well as the salaries of twenty chefs making a living wage. He was famous; he was the toast of the town; but each week when he sat and ran the numbers, he was barely holding on.

And yet for all the compassion and practical understanding I had of who Robuchon was and what he was facing, I was still just nineteen years old. He was my first truly frightening boss. After one month, I was completely terrorized. Even when I could talk myself into letting go of the emotional part of my fear, I would find myself crippled by the mere prospect of trying to match the pace. The amount of work was just too much; even Maurice was struggling to keep up. Sometimes I panicked and asked Gosse to come help in my station, but if Robuchon found fault in one of his dishes, Gosse would simply turn his back on me rather than take responsibility for the slightest mistake.

When I got home at night, I was too tired to brush my teeth. I slept all day Saturday. Sunday I lay in bed with a stomachache, dreading the week ahead while mentally preparing my mise. Monday morning I woke at four to shower and get to work, afraid that I would get there too late to prep in time for lunch.

Sometimes I felt like I didn't understand what Robuchon was asking me to do. The language and techniques were far too advanced. He was very specific about how he wanted, say, the velouté done. Typically a velouté is a light stock thickened with a *roux blond*. But when the first asparagus of the spring came in, Robuchon decided that he wanted to experiment. I was told to cook the stalks in chicken stock, wring them in a towel to extract all the essence, then mix the liquid with cornstarch to bind it. He wanted that sauce combined with crème fraîche and used as the basis for a new dish. I quickly discovered that the cornstarch mixture broke and became liquid, and there was no way I could save it—not that I had the guts to tell him. The sauce also had to be kept over ice until the last minute, because it turned to water the second it hit room temperature. I tried to come up with something similar to what I thought he wanted without him finding out that it wasn't his recipe, until one day the sauce was so thin, the green dots started to dissolve and run into the cream sauce.

I asked a waiter to do me a favor and just send it out. "Please! Don't show it to him! Just take it into the dining room!" I begged.

But the captain saw it and sent it back. He made it clear: he wasn't going to go down for me.

"I don't trust you, Ripert!" I heard the shout from the pass. "You're a liar! How could you lie to me? You already lie about your terrines."

The week before, he'd come over and barked, "Open your fridge!" I couldn't refuse. He pulled out three terrines and slammed them on the counter.

"What in the world are these doing here, Ripert? Are you a magician?"

"Well, it's to feed the staff, Chef! Because we don't want to throw them away." The terrines were actually looking much better, but Robuchon didn't care.

He never had to so much as lift a finger to hurt us: with the strength of his eyes and his attitude, being subject to Robuchon's anger felt like being crucified. "You're lying," he said, his eyes cutting into me. "Now I know why you've been serving this shit for so long. It's because you're cheating. You want to kill my restaurant!"

How had I expected him not to know? This is the man who would look at a scoop of apple on my lobster salad and declare it too white. He could tell at a glance that, in an attempt to get ahead for my service, I'd cut my apples early and dipped them in lemon juice to keep them from browning. How could I have expected him not to catch a premade terrine?

There was no way I could apologize in front of the kitchen. Apologies were never accepted, and they never fixed things.

In Robuchon's kitchen, everything was done just so. You didn't just grab a few mushrooms from the refrigerator and carry them to your station in your apron. Instead, you placed them on a tray and walked to your station carefully, because those mushrooms were sacred. He had an appreciation for quality that bordered on obsession. He believed that flawless raw ingredients were as valuable as the rarest diamonds. He may have ordered only four limes, but they all had to be the exact same perfect size and color. If only one of them was good, the driver for the produce company had to return to Rungis, the major food hall outside of Paris, and come back with ones that matched. If only two of those three were right that time, he would demand a third delivery, and sometimes a fourth.

At La Tour d'Argent, we had beautiful products, but I'd never seen anything like this. Then again, I had never seen a restaurant send a guy back to Rungis four times because the tarragon was not right (first the leaves were too big, then they were too small, and then they were too dark around the edges).

The purveyors must have spent hours going through crates and crates of mushrooms in order to be able to present a basket of ones that were all the same size. Robuchon would order three pounds of carrots and demand that each one be a perfect one-by-six-inch cylinder. He inspected the nails of every chicken to make sure it had been freshly killed, the color of every veal kidney to make sure it wasn't too rosy, the length of the rougets down to the millimeter. But people were so honored to be selling to Jamin (and so afraid to lose the accounts of any of his chefs who'd gone on to cook in big hotels) that they rose to his demands. They respected his encyclopedic knowledge for and love of quality, and it didn't hurt that he would pay any price for the best.

In season, the truffle company Pebeyre from Cahors sent a kilo of black truffles the size of golf balls every single day. In spring, an old woman would show up with a case of morels, and Robuchon would treat her like the queen. He made her feel he was so in love with her mushrooms that it was an honor for him to touch them, a privilege for him to be able to serve them in his restaurant. Every ingredient was a treasure in that kitchen: our job, he reminded us, was to take what was humble and transform it into something noble.

I felt it too. So when he would catch me trying to use Friday's vegetables on Monday, he would yell, "You don't appreciate the product!" because he knew it cut to my heart. I wanted to rise to Robuchon's standards, but taking these kinds of shortcuts was the only way I could stay ahead.

And then, fifteen minutes later, he would start up again: "Ripert! You see? For you it doesn't matter, right? It could be shit."

He was funny that way. Once you'd upset him, he'd keep

coming back at you. An hour later, three days . . . "Why would you do that to a truffle, Ripert? I cannot understand." My wounds were always fresh, because Robuchon never gave anyone time to recover.

I lived for the moments in which he said nothing. Once he'd wiped the rim of one of my plates clean and sent it to the dining room, my stress seemed to melt away. But the alleviation was temporary. Everything at that restaurant had to be perfect, from the service to the food. The final test was when the client sent back the plate. If anything remained, we were all doomed. The waiters knew it. Even the regulars knew it—they made sure to eat every bite.

One day a lobster salad plate caught his eye.

"Ripert, come here! Look at your salad!" I looked at the plate in horror: one piece of lobster and a single dot of apple remained.

"*Oui*, Chef."

"Ah, are you happy with that? Huh? You sabotaged my dish, Ripert! Is this what you wanted?"

"No, Chef." I went back to my station and stayed silent, praying for him to stop.

Five minutes later: "Ripert! How could you do that? How could you send me this lobster salad like that?"

A half hour later: "I cannot believe—I cannot believe the shit you send me! I cannot believe we are serving that to our clients. Where did you learn that shit?"

Even two hours later: "Where did you learn to serve that shit, Ripert? Where did you learn?"

Incredibly, some stations were even more stressful than mine. The poor guy on entremets could never make the perfect mashed potatoes, which probably existed only in Robuchon's mind. One day they would be too starchy, another day too buttery; one day too thin, another day too thick. Too sweet. Too salty. You could tell that the potatoes were becoming an unhealthy obsession for that cook.

There's a reason that line cooks are often so young: the young are more trainable but, more important, they also have the energy to put into the job. Our task was to produce quality and precision for sixteen, eighteen hours a day. There was no Red Bull back then and in Paris, we didn't have Diet Coke, so we powered ourselves up with coffee. I was drinking ten espressos a day. The espresso machine at Jamin was in the back, near my station, and I pumped myself full of double espressos, heavy on the sugar. Like all the other young cooks in the kitchen, I was completely wired. Whatever it took to get the job done.

Because, really, we lived to please Robuchon. His happiness with the food was far more important than the client's: he was a true artist, but to run a team of cooks requires patience as well as vision. We were all challenged ultimately by the demands of Robuchon, but mastering that level of craftsmanship takes years of practice and we didn't have that; we were too young.

We all knew what was driving him. It wasn't anything as base as money: he was determined to get a third star. And his obsession became ours.

20

⋮⋮⋮

Three Stars

Everyone dealt with the pressure differently. Some guys shook all the time. Some went downstairs and cried in the stairwell. I saw a few guys punch the walls. Some guys suffered crippling anxiety attacks.

The only way that we could survive that environment of intensity and rigor was to have a sense of humor. Cooks rarely had time for lunch, but in the late afternoon, when Robuchon went home to have dinner with his family, we had a window to grab coffee at a café. There we made relentless fun of Robuchon. We were obsessed with his status as a Freemason and speculated about all the conspiracy theories. He became this all-knowing, all-seeing being. Was it true that he got so-and-so the job at that big hotel because he's a Mason too? Did he have microphones recording us in the kitchen?

We also vented about some of the petty grievances that drove us nuts. Every day we were required to make dinner for his French poodle, as well as a salad course for his family's dinner, which fell to me, since I was on salads. And every day he called to complain about something: The lettuce had been gritty. His dog didn't finish his dinner because the meat was too tough. What kind of cooks were we that we couldn't even make a meal that a dog would enjoy?

When it came to dealing with the pressure, my chosen coping mechanism was to feign indifference, a technique I had honed during the years of living with my stepfather. I used my body language as a form of passive rebellion. Even when Chef was dressing me down in front of everyone—telling me that I wasn't passionate enough, that I didn't care about the quality, just my little shortcuts—I got as close to him as I could and looked him in the eye, standing straight and proud. No matter how panicked I got, my resolve never wavered. Unlike with Hugo, I couldn't use words to win. But I could draw upon my experience of pretending to be unharmed by abuse— flexible, resilient, and determined to succeed.

I reminded myself of La Fontaine's fable about the oak and the reed. The mighty oak makes fun of the reed for being so scrawny, but the reed doesn't say anything. When a big storm comes and knocks down the oak, the reed bends in the wind and grows back stronger. "See?" he tells the tree. "Now you're broken and I'm still here. I bounce back every time."

Within the team, I had to make believe that I wasn't stressed out. My nickname became the Tourist: I was always the last to arrive in the morning (just fifteen minutes after everyone else, but it didn't go unnoticed) and I would calmly, deliberately make my coffee and toast in a way intended to telegraph that I wasn't in the terror game like them. I was extremely careful never to cut or burn my hands, keeping them impeccable, and to appear as clean and creaseless and relaxed as possible at all times. I hoped that my calm appearance, in addition to the food that I was slowly learning to master, dot by dot, would see me through the service.

I was willing to endure anything just to be able to learn from him. I wasn't there for the money, though he paid us much more fairly than other restaurants. I was there for the passion of cooking and because Robuchon was magnetic: he literally attracted talent. What we were making was so exceptional, so out-there compared to what every other restaurant was doing in terms of presentation and unique flavor combinations, that while I worked I was always thinking, *This is unbelievable.* The quality of the ingredients and the harmony that he created between them was unlike anything I'd ever seen, not to mention the revolutionary visual impact.

I still remember the first time that Robuchon taught me how to make a lobster gelée, which we served carefully layered, caviar first, then the lobster gelée, then cauliflower cream, in a tall Japanese bowl lined with brilliant dots of chlorophyll that I had extracted through a complex process that began with puréeing herbs in the Robocoupe. When I first tasted it, I literally scratched my head and said, "I have never seen or tasted a dish that good in my life." Diners would ask if he had a machine to create such meticulous dots and get them to stay in place just inside the rim of the bowl—they too had never seen anything like it. Neither had anyone in that kitchen. What Joël Robuchon created was terra incognita. It would be years before I'd say the words out loud, but Robuchon—flawed and exacting as he was—was my hero.

Though they were hell to execute, the world was taking notice of the masterpieces Robuchon was thinking up. One afternoon, I noticed he was in an unusually good mood. It was as if the slate of our collective transgressions had been wiped clean and he'd met us each for the first time, and was excited to have us join the team. He patted each of us on the shoulder as we arrived and changed into our kitchen whites. He beamed as he asked us to gather for an important announcement.

"Today I am proud to say that thanks to all of your work, Jamin has just received its third Michelin star," he said, and our band of twenty broke into cheers. "This is the first time in the guide's history that a restaurant has achieved this in just three years."

I don't know who popped the first bottle of champagne, but soon corks were firing like cannons. We were part of culinary history. We had helped Robuchon achieve the near-impossible, becoming one of twenty-two restaurants in France, the restaurant capital of the world, to bear the honor. And in such a short time! At thirty-eight, he was the youngest chef ever to win three stars.

"I would like to reward all of you guys for making it happen. I will have to find a way to celebrate the three stars in style," he said. A few weekends later, he took us all to Burgundy for lunch at a restaurant of one of his protégés. Christophe Cussac had held Maurice's position on the fish station. Now, at his restaurant, L'Abbaye Saint Michel in Tonnerre, he had a Michelin star of his own. We had a fantastic day, eating great food, drinking Chablis, and appreciating the generosity of a man who couldn't possibly have been making that much money yet.

That was the honeymoon. When we returned on Monday, the pressure to keep the three stars turned out to be even more taxing than the pressure to get them. Robuchon was a bit more touchy, but then again, his vision of perfection had never been attainable. He pushed us to our limits to get us to achieve it. We became superhuman in that kitchen, constantly surpassing ourselves. When he told us that he wanted every single pea peeled to reveal the tiny germ inside, we thought it was madness, but we did it. If you were to peel a fresh pea right now, you would see that inside the shell, there is a very tiny sprout attached to every pea. Robuchon wanted us to take off that tiny sprout, because he believed it would add just a hint of bitterness to the dish. When the restaurant's sudden popularity spurred him to open private salons upstairs to accommodate twenty additional guests, we thought it would compromise the quality. But we did it.

Despite the deceptions about the terrine, I believed that I had integrity and dedication, which I hoped that Robuchon could detect. Through relentless hard work and hundreds of thousands of dots over the course of nearly a year, I had developed another level of craftsmanship and precision. (I knew this only because fewer of my dishes were sent back from the pass, and Maurice, now sous-chef, thank God, was sent over to shake his head at me less and less.) Even though I wanted nothing more than to become a great chef like Robuchon, I was terrified of the next step: I would be moved to the next station and have to learn everything all over. And again. And again. I didn't think I could handle it. Not there, at least. The stress had gotten under my skin. I wanted a normal life—not that I knew what that was. But I didn't want to spend my waking hours in fear. I didn't want all of my dreams to involve dots.

My love life was nonexistent. After service, when I should

have been trying to meet women, I was often just sitting in the bar, memorizing some new recipe that Robuchon had thrown my way, working out how to get a better taste for my sauces, wondering how I could plate faster with fewer errors. I could easily spend an hour at the bar, nursing a warm beer, going over the evening's service in my head, wondering where I had gone wrong and how I could make it better. That far-off, glazed look in my eyes, unsurprisingly, did not make me popular with women. If one of my buddies from the restaurant punched me in the shoulder and said, "Hey, Ripert, that girl with the curly hair is looking at you," I could make a move: say hello, buy her a drink, ask her a few questions that might give her the illusion that I was obsessing over something other than how not to get my ass handed to me on a platter at work the next day. But to seal the deal? To wow her, woo her, convince her that she had nothing to lose and everything to gain by taking me to bed that night? That was beyond me. I was too tired, too distracted, too young to be good at that game.

One weekend, a few months after I started work at Jamin, I went home to visit my mother and ran into Madame Amparo.

"Eric, you've grown up!" she said, proudly.

I opened my jacket to show her the necklace she had given me. "I still wear your cross, and I live in a city surrounded by water. You were right."

She nodded. "You will always be happiest surrounded by water. It is where your spirit sails, where you will be most free."

"Madame Amparo, if you ever come to Paris," I promised, "I will make you a meal that you will never forget." I smiled as

I imagined Madame Amparo at Jamin and the predictions she might have for my mercurial boss.

If I ever doubted Madame Amparo's ability, all doubt evaporated as she seemed to read my mind.

"Your boss, he's very tough," Madame Amparo said. "When we look up at the night sky, stars appear to be silver and we imagine them to be cool to the touch. But stars shine bright because they are on fire. The closer you get, the more likely you are to get burned."

I nodded and thought of Robuchon, of his genius and his temper.

"But this is the thing, my child," Madame Amparo continued. "You are headed for the same night sky. When it's your turn to burn brightly, remember where you have been. Be careful not to harm all of those in your orbit."

21

::::

Private Ripert

One spring afternoon, almost a year into my work with Robuchon, I received the letter that every twenty-year-old Frenchman dreads: I was being called for military service. Usually guys tried to get out of it, or managed to get sent somewhere easy or beautiful to serve out their term. I'd been able to delay it for a bit because of my job, but as I read the letter, I realized that I was thrilled to have an excuse to leave. Well, that's not entirely true: I wasn't excited to have my career put on hold just so I could go clown around with guns for a year. But still, it was a break.

When Robuchon came in the next morning, I knocked on his office door and asked if I could sit down. He put down a stack of bills and tried to smile.

"Of course, Eric. What is it? You want to move stations? You think you're ready?"

"No, Chef. I'm sorry, but I've been called to do my military service. I'm giving notice."

His smile disappeared. I could see him calculating. "That's ridiculous. I'll arrange for you to cook at the Elysée. I know the chef there. It will be so easy, cooking for Mitterrand! That way you can stay with us for a little longer." My smile disappeared. If I cooked for the president, I would owe Robuchon. He could force me to come back when my service was finished.

"Actually, I've already been helped by a friend with a good connection," I said as politely as possible. I was hoping to end up in the south of France where the weather would be nice and I'd be only a three-hour drive to Andorra.

"Well, then. You'll finish up here through June?"

"Of course, Chef."

"Congratulations, Eric. I wish you the best."

And with that, I was free. The army was going to be a vacation. When I was finished, I would find another job.

I went home and waited to be called for my military service. I was told it would happen in a week or two, but I got lucky. It was four whole months before I was called. I spent my time home in Andorra, climbing mountains during the day and dancing all night in the local clubs. Sometimes I'd drive a few hours to Barcelona or fly to Ibiza and party there, since the music was better and the chances were higher that one of many dark-haired beauties would talk to me. I was almost twenty, and less shy. I wanted to get all the partying out of my system before going to live in yet another dormitory with a bunch of guys.

I was stationed with the 31st Regiment in Castel Sarrasin, a
pretty little riverfront village near Toulouse. Established in 961,
Castel Sarrasin has a long military history, from being the site of
twelfth-century skirmishes against the British to the Crusades
and the Hundred Years' War. The base was from the 1800s, but
my recently built dormitory reminded me of hotel school.

The point of our service seemed to be more about teaching us to be young men who could follow orders than actually
crafting us into soldiers who could fight in a war. We spent two
months on drills that had no discernible point. We moved piles
of rocks from one side of the road to the other, then back again.
Then we put the rocks in our backpacks and marched miles in
one direction, turned around, and returned.

I tried to point out the stupidity of our exercises, but no
one listened. They'd drop us in a forest and say, "You see those
guys behind the trees over there? That's the enemy. *Attaque!*"

"Wait a minute," I'd interrupt. "They can see me!"

"That's right. You have to find a solution."

"But there's not a solution!" Finally I'd give in. "You want
me to attack? Okay. *On attaque!*" I started running toward
them in the open, my rock-filled pack thumping on my shoulder blades as I tried to hold the gun out in front of me. Inevitably, those of us who weren't blown up by pretend mines
were mowed down by the pretend enemy's guns.

The tasks felt so meaningless that it was hard for me to respect the men giving the orders, or try to learn from what was
being asked of us. They just wanted us to obey, not to think. Okay,
but why did we have to walk together like geese? One-two, one-
two, with half the men unable to keep time while the officers
screamed at us to stay synchronized. Sure, it showed discipline
and organization, but would it really help us win a war?

I liked to provoke the career officers, who were a few years older than us. When I was assigned to guard the munitions at night, I'd wear forbidden civilian clothes, like my mountain-climbing coat from Andorra, under my uniform to stay warm. When we had to go on long marches, I put on my Ray-Bans, blasted David Bowie on my Walkman, and put Ricard in my canteen. (It was so cheap in duty-free Andorra that I brought back six bottles at a time and sold them, when I wasn't offering it around during aperitif hour.)

We spent the first few months on basic training, *les classics*. It seemed like we never stopped cleaning guns, old rifles that were impossible to get clean enough to pass the white-glove test. Whenever an officer held up a greasy, accusing finger and told me that mine wasn't clean, I threw up my grimy hands and said, "What do you want me to tell you? First of all, these guns are from World War II. Second, you have to oil the chamber, so of course your glove is always going to come away with black smudges. Can you tell me how to be a good soldier and a white-glove soldier at the same time, sir?"

The entire base specialized in *génie*, which meant mines, explosives, bridges, and roads. I immediately recognized that the training we were receiving in spotting imaginary mines was a futile undertaking. "Mines are hidden, random, they defy logic," I told my officer. "In a real combat situation, you'd get killed almost instantly."

I was part of the last generation of men in France who served a mandatory military service. At the time, I think the government believed that because you received a free college or vocational education and got free healthcare, mandatory military

service was a way of paying back. In retrospect, I'm happy I
did it. I have the utmost respect for veterans. My paternal
grandfather, Antonin, served in both world wars. My mother's
father, Fernand, was imprisoned in Morocco and escaped the
Germans. But I think as a young kid who served in France
during a time of peace, I didn't really get it.

After the two months of weapons training, because of my
résumé as a chef, I was assigned to the kitchen of the mess. I
was happy to go to the kitchen because the food was pretty
good, and I was looking forward to contributing to that.

On my first day cooking in the mess, my boss announced,
"Today we will make calamari and *sauce Americaine*. Ripert,
you can take care of it."

Sauce Americaine is like a lobster bisque, very technical.
You have to crush the heads of the lobster, for one. But I was
up for it, even excited about it.

Then he handed me a box of frozen calamari. I nodded. It
wasn't ideal, but I'd make it work. This was the military, not
Jamin. I understood that not all of the ingredients I'd be cooking with would be fresh.

"Where are the lobster heads to make the sauce?" I asked.

He shrugged. "Make a béchamel, then add ketchup and
brandy."

I was in shock. Meanwhile, the other cooks in the mess, who
had been tasked with making spaghetti, had managed the unthinkable: they burned the spaghetti while it was cooking in the
boiling water. Because they did not stir the spaghetti, or time it,
the pasta stuck to the bottom of the kettle and burned. I had
never seen—or smelled—anything like it in my life.

I was so horrified that I decided to go and talk to the colonel. He agreed to see me. One of the things I liked about him

from the start was that he was a cool customer, slow to anger, very elegant. I was nineteen years old and I had a mouth on me, so I gave it to him straight. I told him, "I cannot cook shit food the likes of which I have seen today. I'm going to be depressed and get sick. I cannot perform the mess hall duty."

The colonel smiled at me.

I didn't realize how ridiculous I must have sounded, but I was young and I had just come from Robuchon, a place where we worshipped every mushroom, every fava bean, every potato. I believed with all my heart that the appalling behavior passing for cooking that I had witnessed in the mess hall kitchen was a *sacrilege*.

"You don't want to be in the mess hall. Should I send you to the commandos?" He was being sarcastic, but it was lost on me.

"Sir, I can't do the commandos." Those were the guys who were being prepped to fight in the hot spots of the day, Chad and Lebanon. This, needless to say, terrified me. "Look at me!" I said, pointing at my skinny frame. "Do I look like a warrior? A top-secret killer?"

He threw up his hands. "Do you want to be my waiter?"

It was perfect. I waited on him and his guests at lunch and sometimes at dinner in the dining hall above the canteen, which happened to be next to a poultry market. I gave them three-star service—if there had been food to carve tableside or crêpes to flambé, I would have done it happily. Because I worked with a high-ranking officer, I was given privileges that my fellow soldiers envied, like the ability to leave the base after work and get most weekends off. Unfortunately, I still had to go through the program.

Most guys had never experienced discipline like this. For

me, I felt like I was on vacation, just with shorter hair. (And even that I didn't mind. What, they were going to break my spirit by shaving my head? Did that actually work?) Because I'd been a part of a professional kitchen, I understood the hierarchy and discipline of the brigade—and why it's necessary. You work at the level to which you are assigned, performing set tasks within a designated space. You do not think for yourself; you take orders only from the person in charge of your station, and ultimately from the sous-chef, that revered and feared individual who runs the kitchen under the orders of the chef and is the only person allowed to talk during service. Failure to follow orders could result in injury or, worse, a ruined meal. It was just like the military, from which the system was taken. Yet, I have to say that I never felt fully at home during my training.

Back in Andorra, Jacques, who had been Special Forces, seemed to understand my plight completely. "It makes sense that you are bored with your training," he said. "Your battlefield is in the kitchen. The soldiers who know your struggle best are back in Paris, at Jamin."

Waiters and chefs were given special privileges, like being allowed to go out every few nights. I took full advantage of my privileges. My friends and I went to the nightclubs in Toulouse as often as we could to meet college girls, or hung out at Le Sunbeam Café or Le Tout Va Bien restaurant in nearby Moissac. There was a little club along the canal there called Nirvana that played cool music—New Wave, disco, and reggae—where I also spent a lot of time. Soldiers weren't allowed there, but with my silk Smalto shirt, ultraslim Levi's cuffed at the ankle, and Sebago leather loafers, no one thought I was from the barracks.

One night, a girl came up to me and said, "I know who you are. You're Eric Ripert." I thought, *Who is this girl? She's not even flirting with me.*

"My name is Patricia. I have to introduce you to your sister. You look like twins."

"My sister's in Andorra with my mother," I said, turning to walk away.

"No, your father's daughter. We're friends; she lives nearby."

I was shocked. My half sister was six months old when my father died. When Francine, my stepmother, disappeared, she'd taken my sister with her, and I'd never heard from them since.

"Do you want to meet her?" Patricia asked.

I did.

The next weekend, I went to the Café de Commerce, a little place in Moissac owned by a guy we all knew and liked named Fissou, to meet Stéphanie. It was like looking at the female version of myself. No, more than that: it was like looking into my father's eyes again. For the first few minutes, we were both too moved to speak. I felt like the shocked eleven-year-old crying in my room in Andorra. Eventually, we started talking. "I grew up around here," she told me. When Francine ran after my father's death, she and her daughter ended up in Moissac, where Francine married another bank director. There was some real estate that hadn't been settled—apartments my father owned around St. Tropez—so my grandfather had gotten fed up and hired a private detective to track down Francine and get what was owed to me. But I had been protected from all of that, so I never knew that this was where she lived, and I would never have guessed that one day I would live in a barracks a few kilometers away.

Stéphanie had no memory of our father, so I told her about his gardening and his jazz, his vinegar making and his trumpet playing, how much fun he was to be around, and how sad I was to have lost him so young. I couldn't resist asking if her mother was still a terrible cook. Marika was, in my mind, so closely paired with Hugo that it was difficult to feel close to her. Stéphanie, who was my father's daughter, who looked so much like me, was like the sister I never had.

Patricia was thrilled to have been able to connect us, and it turned out that she had another girl she wanted me to meet, this one a colleague at the gift shop where they worked across from the Café de Commerce.

Bernadette was petite and curvy. She was what we call *chatain*, with hair that was a beautiful ombre color between brown and blond. Even though she had a certain maturity and sophistication, I could tell right away that she wasn't used to going out to clubs or having twenty-year-olds flirt with her. Maybe that was because she was only eighteen, but she intrigued me much more than the knowing, made-up girls who were outgoing enough to make the first move. When a slow dance came on, for once I wasn't feeling shy. I took a chance and kissed her. She kissed me back with such passion that I called her the next afternoon and the next.

Working at Jamin I felt I could never get it right, but during those early days with Bernadette, I felt I could do no wrong. To her, my opinions were always the worldliest and best thought out. She laughed at my jokes and took my proclamations about life and politics as encyclopedic fact. I was just a few years older than her, but I spoke French and Spanish. I had lived and worked in Paris. She thought I was sophisticated and worldly, and I loved the reflection of myself that she presented.

Before I knew it, I was spending the night at her parents' farmhouse (me in one bedroom, her in the next), and speeding back to the base before I had to serve breakfast. Her parents were conservative, and they pretended not to hear the old farmhouse floorboards creak as I crept into her room at night and back again in the morning.

I liked being around her family. Bernadette's mother, Denise, was an orphan who had been hired as a maid in the home of a rich man. Her boss, Georges, was one of the biggest fruit farmers and landowners in Moissac, an agricultural region famous for its fruit and sunflowers. He treated Denise like family, so when she got married, he sold her one of his neighboring houses at a price she and her husband, a *fonctionnaire,* could afford. Bernadette and her brother, Jean-Claude, referred to Georges as their uncle. Denise was warm and gracious. Her father liked me too, and he was always telling some sort of tall tale about the elusive game he'd shot and enormous fish he'd caught. I just nodded and went along with the tales as I ate Denise's delicious food, which she made with ingredients from the surrounding fields. Jean-Claude was about five years older than me. He was an attorney and was very strict with his little sister. He wanted Bernadette to study and do well in school and get into a university, even though she wasn't interested. Jean-Claude saw me as the distraction that I was; he was courteous to me, but nothing more.

After Bernadette and I had been dating for a few weeks, her family took me with them next door to have Sunday lunch chez Georges. I remember thinking that his tall stone and brick house wasn't as grand as I expected for someone who owned more than three hundred acres. The door opened right into the kitchen, which was centered around a formidable antique table with elaborately carved legs, at which one of the housekeepers was peeling potatoes for the deep fryer.

I could tell from the smoke coming out of an adjoining house that most of the cooking was being done over there, in the fireplace. When I stepped into the winter kitchen, which was obviously in use all year, my breath caught. On one side was a massive wooden refrigerator from the 1920s. A meat slicer sat on a counter nearby, a silver platter layered with thin slices of sausage and ham balanced on top. But the focal point of the room was the wide, blackened fireplace with an automated spit where chickens were roasting. On the unembellished mantel, between a row of antique jars, wooden crosses, and statues of the Virgin Mary, rested a forgotten juice glass of wine.

Georges smiled as I came in. He tipped off his bowler hat, straightened his raggedy brown cardigan, and grabbed my hand. The connection was immediate.

"This is the great chef from the city?" he said with his strong southern accent. "Come! You must help me carve the birds. I killed them myself! I wish you'd been here to help me pluck them. But look at your hands: they're much too soft for a cook's—or a soldier's."

He was tall and slim, with white hair and mischievous blue eyes, like a little boy's. All the youth and vitality that defined him could be seen in his face: the eyes that were always laughing and the sly, sideways grin when he made a joke, which was often. His voice boomed with that unmistakable Gascony accent with its big R's: every R in *eve-R-y wo-Rd* was articulated. There was a singsong quality to the rhythm of speech in that area, and when Georges spoke, it sounded like music.

He raised his hands to show me his meaty, gnarled fingers. "You need a little farm life to toughen you up! Next month, come help us pick artichokes. Then you'll know what country life is all about. We farmers might not be smart like you, but we can teach you something."

As we prepared dinner for Georges's guests (a mixture of friends and family from the surrounding town), I sliced up two of the birds while Georges hacked at the others with a battered cleaver. I could tell that he was only pretending to be clumsy; to my eye, he took great pride in the food. The family gathered under the shade of the chestnut tree in the little gravel courtyard outside the cooking house, where we spent the rest of the afternoon eating and drinking, our voices rising and our laughter increasing with each platter that was carried out of the house. Georges proudly told me about the provenance of each antique and where he'd found it. Between courses, he had me kneeling in front of a cabinet in the living room and looking through box after leather box of ebony-handled knives, hefty silver serving spoons, and elaborate salad forks. "Not bad for a farmer, eh?" he asked with a wink.

His lighthearted humor and outgoing southern warmth reminded me of my grandparents in Nice and put me completely at ease. Even from that one meal, I could tell that he knew about good ingredients in a way that would impress even Robuchon. By the time his daughter, Monique, brought out a warm tart made with just-picked apricots, I felt as though I had been adopted. I wanted to spend every Sunday cooking in the fireplace with Georges.

It had been a long time since I had felt so at home with a family. My father would have loved Georges, I was sure of it. My father was not a real *paysan;* he was a Sunday farmer in his little garden. But his parents had been farmers, and although my father was a sophisticated bank president who loved fast cars and beautiful women, there was a part of him that prized the simple pleasures of life above all else. As I sat at the fireplace with Georges, many of my most beloved memories of my father came rushing back: My father changing from his suit to a T-shirt and khakis and tending to the vegetables in our backyard. My father teaching me how to swim in the ocean and how to gallop a horse at faster and faster clips through the woods. My father grilling kabobs by the beach in St. Tropez. The country fireplace in Gascony and the beach fires my father made were different, but the warmth was the same.

22

::::

A Return to the Madman

A few weeks before I was set to be discharged, a clerk approached me. "Ripert, you've got a message."

I looked down at the scrap of paper and the familiar phone number. Robuchon.

No way, I thought. *This guy is fucking with me.* Even with his Masonic superpowers, there was no way Robuchon could have found me in Castel Sarrasin. How did he know?

I called Joël Robuchon from the phone booth on the base.

"Hello, Chef. What a surprise!"

"Hi, Eric, how are you? Did you like your military service?"

He told me about some of the goings-on at the restaurant.

He'd undertaken a small renovation and he was looking forward to my seeing it. Then finally he got to the matter at hand. "Listen," he told me, "I need a chef poissonier. Are you interested?"

I was stunned. Whatever I expected Robuchon to say, it wasn't that. "Chef poissonier? But, Chef, I was only on garde manger! I can't make hot sauces yet. Not the complicated—"

"Eric, you can do it. We'll teach you."

"Um, I have to think about it." I could already feel the familiar sense of panic swelling in my chest.

"Of course you can think about it. You have one minute."

I couldn't go back. There was no way. If I had to go back, I would die. Or kill someone. Or at least have a nervous breakdown. And yet . . . Robuchon didn't call just anyone. This was a huge honor. My terror was joined by pride. Even though I knew I wasn't the best cook in Robuchon's kitchen, he thought I could do it, which must mean that he saw some talent. Besides, I began to reason, the fish station was the most interesting one at Jamin, at least in my opinion and taste as well. I thought what he was doing with fish was so incredible and refined. The sauces and garnishes were so complex and varied, they made my rabbit terrine seem like a roast chicken with a sprig of parsley. Oh, God. I had never done hot sauce at Jamin! Even Maurice could barely make it through service some nights. I would never survive. *Come on. Be realistic. Save yourself! Tell him no. You may never work in Paris again, but at least you'll be sane.*

If I learned fish and sauce from Robuchon, I would be able to do pretty much anything I wanted after that. Robuchon was impossible, but he was an impossible genius, and I wanted—needed—to learn from the best. What stayed with me, night after exhausting night, was the criticism, but I knew that he would not have called me out if he didn't believe I was capable. The kind and joking voice on the phone did not fool me this time. Life at Jamin would continue to be a living hell, but I would learn—a lot.

"When do I start?"

All I could think about was ending things with Bernadette. The relationship was becoming more challenging because Bernadette was young and prone to jealousy, and I was so focused on my career. A plan began to take shape: I would tell her that I was going back to work in Paris, and that she had to stay and finish lycée. I would promise to come back next summer, saying that we'd figure out what to do then. Or better yet: I was being sent to Chad as a secret commando. We must never speak again, for the security of the country. . . .

Her brother had another suggestion: over breakfast a few weeks before the end of my service, he leaned close and whispered, "Bernadette's jealousy is consuming her. The two of you will never work. Just leave. We won't tell her where you've gone." I knew he was right, and I should have accepted his help. But I still liked Bernadette, and there was something about her that I found hard to let go.

Then, right before I finished my military service, I went to a movie in Toulouse. The film was *An Officer and a Gentleman*. At the end, all of the officers leave their girlfriends behind when they change bases, callously breaking the women's hearts. But not the hero. He blows back into town on a motorcycle because he can't live without the woman he loves. It seems so silly now, but I left the theater inspired. So much so that I developed a serious case of amnesia regarding the dynamic of our relationship. I decided that I wasn't going to leave my girlfriend, making her just another jilted sweetheart in a military base town. Instead, I invited her to come live with me back in Paris. I was twenty-one, Bernadette was nineteen, and we were playing house in an uninsulated, definitely illegal plywood shack that had been rigged together on top of an old apartment building next to the Porte de Versailles. (I told my mother it was a penthouse.) It meant a serious commute to the restaurant, but it was all I could afford.

5:55 A.M. The dread returned before I even pressed the intercom button marked JAMIN. Now that I was here, I couldn't fathom why I had ever agreed to come back. Did I really think that, after more than a year away from the line, I could cook fish for Robuchon?

From my first day back at Jamin, I knew that I was doomed. At the restaurant, I recognized quite a few of the faces in the locker room, including Eric LeCerf, my friend from garde manger; Benoît Richard, who'd been the chef on meats when I was there; and of course Maurice, who was now running the kitchen at Jamin.

My stomach tightened when I heard Robuchon's car pull into the garage at nine. Then a few minutes later, an affectionate slap on the back of the head. "Eric! I see you have returned to the fold. Bienvenue! You have much to learn. Philippe Braun here will be teaching you everything you need to know about fish. It's not like garde manger, where you had a week or two of instruction. No. You and Philippe will be working closely together for the next three months. Perhaps by then you will begin to understand. *Bonne chance*."

And so my education began. Robuchon was determined to offer the diners the best quality and freshest product available. The fish we cooked was so expensive, Robuchon ordered only as much as was needed for the day, and even then it often ran out. The waiters were under strict instructions to make sure that none of it went to diners who might not appreciate it. With a shudder, I remembered a night during my first stint at Jamin. We were down to just six portions of rouget left when a table of five Texans decided to give it a try.

"They're not going to eat it," Robuchon snapped at the captain when he saw their ticket. "Rouget is too fishy for Americans. I don't want them to have it. Tell them to order something else."

A few minutes later, the captain returned, pale and trembling, to apologize. As hard as he'd tried to convince them, the gentleman ordering for the table insisted.

"If they don't eat it, you will see," said Robuchon. We braced ourselves.

Five beautiful plates of rouget went out. Four beautiful plates of rouget returned, barely touched. The captain tried to imitate the Texan's voice as he shrugged his shoulders and said, "Don't worry about it! I'll pay for it." This poor tourist had no idea what the waiter and the kitchen were about to endure.

"You see! I told you, but you didn't understand a word!" he barked at the captain. "Look at this fish! Now what do we do? Do you know how much this fish cost? Do you?" The captain hung his head and practically crawled back to the dining room.

Despite the fact that the client paid for the fish, Robuchon was distraught. He hated not pleasing the client. He hated that the beautiful, expensive pieces of fish were going straight into the garbage. For him, it was a failure coming and going.

"What do we do with the fish?" Robuchon cried every half

hour for the rest of the night. "Why don't you ever listen?" he said each time the waiter came in to pick up a plate.

The fish dishes weren't as technically exhausting as the ones I'd labored over on garde manger, but the cooking required a precision that was much more harrowing. And the sauces, well, it would be months before I was allowed to make those on my own.

For the first few weeks, I watched and worked with a mixture of fear and determination as Philippe Braun, the current chef poissonier, did his work. Robuchon respected Philippe because he came from a culinary family. Philippe's uncle owned a famous three-star Michelin restaurant called Au Crocodile in Strasbourg. What I liked about Philippe was that he was very artistic, almost poetic, in his description of the sauces. He would explain that some sauces were very masculine—bold flavors, dense in texture. Other sauces were more feminine—subtle, delicate, refined. For so long, my time with Robuchon had been about executing the boss's vision. But with Philippe, I began to see that you could still have a vision of your own. It was up to each of us to imbue the work with our own meaning and style.

The fish station was, in the most ideal circumstances, manned by three guys. Philippe was in charge. He handled the most delicate elements of the fish station and was the master of the sauces. The sauce is everything. It's hard to learn how to make a sauce—to capture flavors in a liquid and anticipate how they will behave requires a lot of craftsmanship. What will expand? What will fade? It's a process, and it takes a long time before you can play with flavors and really begin to execute the magic of making the sauce. During that year after my military service, Philippe was slowly mentoring me on the art of the sauces.

As his second in command, my job was to cook the fish—under Philippe's supervision—and to prepare the garnishes. Philippe, as the head of the station, plated each dish, but I was there to help him.

Depending on the season and staffing, there was sometimes a third guy under me—a commis who did some of the prep and helped keep the station clean.

I immediately understood why garde manger was considered vacationland compared to being on the line. The fish station worked at a constant disadvantage, since the fish was the last delivery to arrive each morning. We had practically no time to clean and fillet it. Once the orders came in, we almost always had to get help on our station to keep up, which meant that we had even less room in which to work.

Philippe showed me what I would be responsible for making: two sauces with lobster, one with shrimp, another with verjus, and a few other complex sauces, including a fennel sauce, a lobster coral emulsion, bouillons, and more mise en place. Once again, I found myself being pushed to my limits to deliver impossible things. Each of the eight or nine sauces had to be made fresh twice a day, which demanded endless cutting and slicing. I couldn't have kept up if I hadn't prepared some of my mise for dinner while getting ready for lunch, hiding it in the back of my fridge. When it got really busy, I sometimes saved a little bit of the sauce from lunch for dinner. But Robuchon could always tell.

"Is it fresh?" he would ask, reaching for a tasting spoon.

"Yes, Chef. I just did it."

The lids of his eyes drew halfway down as he frowned. "You're a liar. Do it again."

Sometimes my deceptions would have been comical had they not felt so vital. One day I was supposed to be making a saffron sauce for canapés, but Philippe hadn't taught it to me yet. He was downstairs having a cigarette when I heard: "Eric! *Fais-moi goûter la sauce du canapé.*"

Shit, I thought. *What am I going to do? I have nothing. Okay. It will take Philippe three minutes to have his smoke . . .*

"*Oui,* Chef!" I yelled from my corner.

"So, aren't you going to get a pan?" Robuchon asked.

"*Oui, oui,* Chef!" I grabbed a saucepan and a whisk and started moving the whisk back and forth in the empty pot. Clack-clack-clack! Where the hell was Philippe?

"*Alors,* is your sauce coming or not?" Chef inquired.

"Chef, one more minute!" Clack-clack-clack.

"That's enough! I want to see your sauce."

Philippe was nowhere to be seen. I didn't have the courage to say that I didn't know how to make the sauce.

"Come here and show me!"

I moved through quicksand, bringing him the shiny-bottomed pot.

"How could you do such a thing?" he said. "Do you know nothing? Has Philippe taught you nothing? Why are you such a liar, Ripert? You with your fake terrines and your ghost sauce?"

It was always like this. He called me Eric when my work was tolerable, but it was Ripert when he was mad. And, man, was he obsessed with the rabbit terrine I had ruined almost three years before. As for the ghost sauce, it was aptly named, because Robuchon would no doubt make sure that story followed me to my grave.

When I sent dishes to the pass, I heard my share of "*ça va pas du tout,* Ripert. Take it back." After a few months, though, Robuchon began to say nothing when he saw my plates—that golden silence! I thought I might finally be getting the hang of it, until the night I saw one of my entrées return to the kitchen.

My heart fell through the floor. It looked nicely cooked, but the one piece that had been cut away showed the fillet to be raw.

Worse: Robuchon had let it go out to the dining room.

"Who made this fish?" he asked with an eerie calm.

"I did, Chef." He took the plate from me and I thought he was going to smash it over my head. But Robuchon was never violent with us. He rarely even swore.

He threw the fillet into a pan and slammed it on the stove.

"Did you see that? Bravo!" he shouted.

No one in the kitchen was breathing.

"That's excellent. Ex-cel-lent! Did you see? It's raw!" and then he went into his office and slammed the door. I finished cooking the fish and sent it back to the pass, where Maurice was standing there, shaking his head. I couldn't meet his eye.

Two hours later, Robuchon returned to drive the point home again: "Did you see that? It's not good! It's raw!"

An hour later, he came back and screamed it again. "Raw!"

This went on for weeks, an endless loop of disappointment and indignation.

The kitchen was set up so that each station faced Robuchon, who stood on an elevated platform, almost like a conductor stands over an orchestra in the pit of a theater. Each dish had to pass his watchful eye before making it out to the dining room. At my station there was a big work table where I would do the day's prep. It was a stainless steel table and the drawers beneath were refrigerated so I could keep the ingredients nearby and cold. The stove where I cooked each day was actually behind me. Standing with my back to Robuchon did a number on my nerves like you wouldn't believe. From where Robuchon stood, he could watch your every move and you never knew where he was. He could be standing at his perch, like an eagle ready to swoop in for the kill. He could be over in pastry, paying you no mind at all. Or he could be hovering right over your shoulder, about to snap at you for overcooking the expensive *loup de mer*. Part of the peace of the early morning was that Robuchon was not in the building yet. I could face forward and prepare my mise en place and hope that today was a day where my mistakes were so minor that he focused his ire elsewhere.

The relentless fear and intensity of our environment began to transform us mentally. Once I saw a chef heat his tasting spoon over an open flame and then hold it against his cook's hand to punish him for not doing his job correctly. Some guys would come up behind you and kick you in the ankles. Fear creates fear, and cruelty follows. But Joël never knew; he would never have accepted such atrocities.

Philippe never cowered under the pressure. He was the French chef equivalent of a California surfer dude, always laid back and ready to enjoy the thrill of the ride. Although I didn't see it at the time, Philippe's passion, focus, and Zen-like attitude would have a long-term effect on both my career and life. He loved making sauces. He liked beautiful women. Outside of that sacred dyad, nothing much got under his skin. He was immune to Robuchon's rants largely because he was so good at his job that he gave Robuchon very little material for the cutting remarks that were his main weapons. But even when Robuchon managed to find fault in one of Philippe's dishes, he never collapsed under the criticism. I longed for Robuchon's approval and when I didn't get it, I felt crushed under the weight of his disappointment. Philippe was different. He was confident enough that he could separate the useful part of the critique from the withering abuse that Robuchon heaped on top, then go back and make the dish better.

My time with Philippe was important because he wasn't just teaching me how to cook: he was teaching me how to be. When you're on the line, every shift is a fight to the end. Handling forty covers at Jamin felt like twelve rounds in a boxing ring. Sometimes you knocked it out, sometimes you went down in the third. Either way, you took your blows and you went home at night, bruised and exhausted. It's hard—nearly impossible—to see the big picture when you're a young chef because all the orders coming at you, and all the technical intricacies you must master, they feel like a punishment. But when your time finally comes to be in charge, when you get to call the shots and it's your job to make a kitchen full of young up-and-comers execute plate after plate of flawless dishes, you draw from all of your training. You think of all those who bossed you, trained you, frightened you, impressed you, and you must decide: How will you act?

Philippe planted a seed in me that would take years to fully form: that maybe there was a way to lead without using anger and fear as the primary tools. Maybe I could love the sauces, love the ladies, love my life—the way Philippe did. Maybe there was a way to control the heat so that, like Philippe, I could keep my cool.

The pressure of working for Robuchon was taking its toll and too often the stress of work followed me home. At least once a week I awoke from a nightmare in which I had screwed up my mise and Robuchon was about to open my fridge. One night, after a particularly rough service, I came home, took one look in the refrigerator and yanked Bernadette out of bed.

"Look at this fridge!" I yelled. "Look at this fucking mess! I want you to fix it right now. How can you be so disorganized? Who treats their lettuces like that? What did you do to my mushrooms?"

She stared at me in frightened disbelief. "You're going crazy!" she said, beginning to cry. "What's happening to you at that place?"

What was happening was that I was losing it. And so were the guys in the kitchen around me. We were buckling under the pressure and the constant barrage of criticism, and we were becoming mean. No matter where I was, I felt like I was constantly under siege.

Bernadette was miserable as well. She wasn't used to living in the city and stayed alone in the apartment all day. The only time she left or spent time with anyone else was on the weekends when we saw Maurice and his girlfriend, or went to the occasional neighborhood bistro. Even if she'd been comfortable enough to go to a great restaurant, we couldn't afford to eat there, since I spent all my money on rent, métro tickets, and groceries. For me, there was no such thing as a sandwich or a bowl of spaghetti on the weekend. When I cooked at home, I shopped for the same quality of ingredients that my mother or Robuchon would buy, and always prepared an appetizer, entrée, and dessert, which meant that our little dinners ended up being much more expensive than dining out. Finally, after a year, we moved to a slightly better place in the 13th arrondissement and Bernadette got a job working at a hotel trade magazine, which helped for a while.

Before my military service, Robuchon had decided that we were using too much butter, so he posted a book on the pass. We had to sign out for each slice of butter we cut from the giant block that in French is called *motte de beurre*. Then, I guess because he thought we were spending too much time in the restroom, he put a red bathroom book outside of his office. We were to sign in and out for bathroom breaks. *Libération,* a Paris newspaper, got wind of the "pee-pee book" and made fun of Robuchon, so the books disappeared.

A few months after I returned from my military service, the bathroom book reappeared. It seemed crazy to me, knowing how hard we all worked, how we needed every second to get the service right, that he might think that we'd waste time in the bathroom. But there it was, a log to keep track of how we spent our time in the loo. You had to write down what time you went into the bathroom and what time you returned to your station. I thought it was bullshit, so I started penciling things like:

Ripert / 8:55 pee-pee /8:57, bring back the key
Ripert / 11:00 am caca / 11:03, bring back the key

It seemed like such a small thing, but I wanted him to know that things had changed since my military service. I wasn't a kid anymore. He never said anything about my insouciant comments, but a few days later, the log disappeared for good.

A year into my second stint at Jamin, Philippe Braun took another job and Robuchon announced that I had been promoted to the saucier for the fish station. It was an honor, but I was paralyzed by the thought of what lay ahead. It was a really tough, physical job, making a series of complex recipes from scratch twice a day. Robuchon was especially demanding of his sauces, and while they relied upon strict technique, which I'd learned at La Tour d'Argent, what made them great could not be taught. You can't truly measure ingredients for a perfect sauce—there's no such thing as an inch of rosemary flavor. It's in your head and in your palate, and the only way to get there is through experience. Consistency and color alone require years and years (and years) to master. I knew that it would be at least a full year before I would start to get the hang of it.

I was promoted to Philippe's position, but things didn't get better or easier. The sauces were hard to master and my instinct for assembling flavor in a delicate liquid form was still developing. In the fish station, you had to be extremely cautious. Fish, by nature, is delicate. Time is of the utmost importance. You can braise a piece of meat for fifteen minutes and it's no tragedy, but that would ruin a piece of fish.

When I became the head of the fish station, I was struggling so much each day and with each dish that I could never have imagined that fish would eventually become my specialty, my passion. But even then, amid all the stress, there were moments of fascination: I was intrigued by how delicate it was, how refined the sauce and garnish had to be to enhance the quality and flavor of the fish. I grew to love how cautious you had to be with technique in order to cook the fish well, and how essential timing was.

It wasn't that I fell in love with a particular style of cooking, a dish, or an ingredient. But there is a way of working with fish that began to speak to me. Cooking meat brings the soul out of you; when you cook a steak or a stew, you don't have to be so precise. But fish brings elegance out of you. You must be intensely focused, and you have to use all your knowledge to elevate the fish.

The fish station was where Robuchon was more innovative, less tied to classicism. The way Escoffier was cooking meats is much the same way we cook meat today. The way Escoffier was cooking fish? That way of cooking is now totally obsolete. He would cook a piece of salmon for two or three hours. Robuchon and his generation of chefs obliterated the old thinking about fish. We barely cook salmon now; we are very cautious and gentle. That was all new when I was the fish chef at Jamin, and that was exciting.

My assistant in the fish station was a talented young chef named Guillaume Brahimi. We had a good dynamic together. He was smart, a strong line cook, and loyal. Unlike in many other stations, Guillaume and I had each other's back. When Robuchon found our plates lacking and began to berate us, we didn't throw each other under the bus.

Once I began to run the fish station and plating the dishes became my supervisory responsibility, I began to understand that cooking is not about architecture first. It's about the flavor and harmony of the ingredients you put into each dish. Robuchon presented these almost 3-D plates with complex mosaics of color and ingredients and yes, he was pushing the design to the limit. But he was always thinking about the flavor first. The painting was the food and the flavors. The presentation on the plate was the frame.

Every kitchen shapes you, and with Robuchon what I learned was attention to detail, rigor, passion for beauty, precision, and discipline. It was craftsmanship at its finest. There was, at the time, no creativity on my part; I was just duplicating his vision. But in duplicating a dish like the fanned baby red mullet with an olive oil emulsion and tempura-fried celery leaves, I learned through imitation what I could not have learned in any other kitchen in Paris.

The whole kitchen staff got a reprieve when Robuchon took an extended trip to Japan. Things were so peaceful when he was away—busy and intense, yes, but it was so much easier to focus on making sure my execution was perfect without his intimidating presence. And then suddenly he was back, determined to sashimi our egos down to size.

"You think you guys are champions and that you are the best because you work in a three-star restaurant." He stalked around the kitchen, making sure to lock eyes with each and every one of us. "You all suck! In Japan, the chefs are ten times better than you. They're more humble than you. They are more skilled, more precise, more gifted. Better, better, best! They are better, and they are the best!" It was crushing at the time, but when I traveled to Japan myself years later, I understood. In Japan, the restaurants had the precision and the unerring commitment to excellence he was always aiming for. It was his dream: the Japanese perfection of Western cuisine.

Robuchon was one of the first chefs in France to be influenced, and mesmerized, by Japanese cooking. And it's perhaps in his cuisine that the Asian influence has been felt the greatest. That influence was mostly felt in the fish station. In technique and in presentation, Jamin began to represent a bridge between French culture and Japanese culture. Robuchon was creating that bridge and we were all a part of it.

Though fear and pressure in some ways defined my time at Jamin, there was also a tremendous amount of pride in working there. It took months to get a reservation, and just to say that you worked with Robuchon was like saying you played guitar for a world-famous rock band: people didn't necessarily know you, but they knew you were big-time.

By the time I returned to Jamin, I was twenty-two, and I knew that I was receiving the best possible training for the levels of cooking I dreamed of doing. And yet, each Sunday my stomach would start churning with anxiety. I would feel too sick to eat. I didn't sleep Sunday nights because my brain was flooded with fear about everything that might go wrong. Starting a new station from zero was taking its toll. Each night, when I thought I was going to die (or lose my mind), I would begin counting the hours until I could leave: "Okay, it's seven now. Even if he keeps us here until one, that's only six hours, max! I can do it."

I knew I still wanted to get to the top of the mountain, but I couldn't see it anymore. I put my head down and staggered ahead. Through repetition and determination to be great (or at least better than good), I began to understand the sauces I was preparing. I started to allow myself to feel my way through them, not just assemble them by rote. I knew when a sauce I had made was delicious—perfectly balanced and deeply flavored. And if I was lucky, Robuchon would choose that moment to demand a taste. Benoît Richard knew that my sauces had finally gotten there, but he wanted Robuchon to think that he constantly had to help me out. He wanted the credit for my hard work. One of my worst moments at Jamin was when, after hearing the chef call for my foie gras truffle sauce, Benoît ran over, grabbed my pan when Chef's back was turned, and brought it to the pass himself.

"*Ah, Benoît. Ça c'est de la sauce,*" he said, his expression temporarily slackened with pleasure. "*C'est délicieux.*" In that kitchen, it was the highest praise anyone could ever hope for. And I never got it.

When Robuchon was upset with me, he'd say, "You'll never be a saucier." It was like a knife in the heart. Never mind the irrationality of it—I *was* the saucier on the fish station!—I was desperate for him to recognize my progress. "You have it or you don't," he would tell me. "Too bad you don't."

Day after day, my life in that kitchen was like a psychological experiment to determine the precise combination of pressure, pain, and fear it takes to make someone lose it completely. We weren't afraid of physical violence. It was purely psychological—a heavy torrent of bad weather that never let up, making you doubt whether clear skies existed at all. Robuchon wasn't a pan thrower like so many chefs of his generation, nor did he curse like them. Instead, we were terrified of disappointing him, of hitting the switch that caused him to spend hours going over our failures again and again, striking our weak spots until we were raw with shame.

Some chefs survived by taking credit for others' work. I strove to be one of the most laid-back in the group, but even I could be extremely selfish about my comfort in that kitchen. I began to look out only for myself: if my commis made a mistake, well, he was on his own. We were all hard on our commis because we were always afraid, and cruelty is one of fear's most common by-products. It would take me a very long time to unlearn those methods of surviving under pressure.

Some chefs simply couldn't handle it. There was a kid who

came to Jamin from Alain Chapel, one of the most revered restaurants in France at the time. He never made it past his training on garde manger. Already skinny to begin with, he had no time to eat and he was too stressed out to sleep when he went home. On his second Friday, he fainted and fell down the stairs. By the following Wednesday, he was gone.

One of the guys we worked with, who had struggled with depression, tried to commit suicide. I wasn't on the edge myself, but I knew that something bad was happening to me at Jamin. I was, increasingly, beaten down and frustrated, miserable and angry. But Robuchon was king and I could not imagine leaving him. And yet, I didn't know how it would ever get better if I stayed.

23

America

Bernadette's constant jealousy only compounded the stress I felt at my job. I would come home from a seventeen-hour day at the restaurant and she would accuse me of having spent the evening in some girl's bed. I began to forget what it was like when we first got together—how lucky I'd felt to have such a beautiful girl be so head over heels for a guy like me.

Most nights when I came home, I was too tired to defend myself. Bernadette would take my silence as a confession, getting more and more worked up until she would start throwing at me whatever she could get her hands on: glasses, plates, books, bottles. It was exhausting, and I didn't have the time or the ability to give her the attention and reassurances she needed.

When Bernadette and I finally moved into a better apartment, Maurice and his wife came to help us with the heavy lifting. To this day, Maurice still talks about carrying my sofa up five flights of stairs because my new apartment had no elevator! But what I remember most from that time was how in love Maurice and his wife were. How she always seemed to encourage him and believe in him and how every decision, from which jobs they would take to how they would spend the holidays, was undertaken as if they were equal members of a team. Maurice's wife, Brigitte, was beautiful and the attraction between them was clear, but what impressed me most was the deep sense of trust and friendship. I wanted to have that in my own relationship, and I began to doubt that I ever could with Bernadette.

A few days later, I sat Bernadette down and told her that maybe she needed to go back to Moissac for a while. We were making each other miserable. Besides, she hated Paris. She needed the country and to be around her family.

Miraculously, she agreed. Under one condition: "I want you to promise that you'll never leave me," she said, crying. "I'm going to tell Maurice to keep an eye on you. Maybe you could stay with him while I'm gone?"

"Whatever makes you happy. And I'll tell Georges to keep an eye on you to make sure you don't run away with a handsome soldier that you pick up at Le Nirvana." It was meant as a joke, but she just nodded at me solemnly.

Even with Bernadette gone for a few weeks, I was breaking down at work. The only thing that got me through was the awareness that my skills were getting stronger. Each sauce was a struggle, but one that I could work through with increasing confidence.

I still hid a little bit of everything I needed to have ready as backup in case Robuchon decided my sauce was shit just before service, and because I had to be prepared when inspiration struck. Out of the blue one morning, he decided he wanted to try something new. So he asked me to prepare a bunch of cockles for him. I steamed the cockles in the couscoussier and brought them to him.

"Where is the jus?" he asked.

"The jus?" He hadn't mentioned it. In fact, he hadn't mentioned anything, just said, "Prepare these."

"The jus! Why didn't you steam them and save the jus?"

I would have saved the jus if he had explained just a little bit more what he was looking for. But he hadn't asked for the jus, he'd asked me to steam cockles without explaining the purpose of the task. I tried to explain this, but he just cut me off.

"Why are you always sabotaging me?" And off he went. Forty-five minutes later, he'd escalated to screaming. "Have you no respect for the product?" He knew I worshipped those ingredients, but he kept jabbing me exactly where I was most sensitive. Finally, I couldn't take it anymore.

Underneath my breath, I said, "Shut the fuck up, asshole."

I didn't mean for him to hear me, but he did. "What did you say?" he asked, looking at me incredulously.

I looked at the ground and said nothing.

"Repeat what you said!" he bristled, challenging me.

Again, I said nothing.

He was sputtering now, in shock and furious because no one ever, ever talked back to Robuchon.

"If you're not happy, Ripert, just say the word," he said.

I thought about it for a second and for the first time, I answered truthfully.

"I'm not happy." I took my apron off and handed it to him.

I walked all the way to the end of the kitchen, every second lasting an hour. As I got to the top of the stairs to the locker room, I wondered what the hell I was doing. In that kitchen, we all believed that Robuchon was God: He knew everything there was to know about cooking. He knew everything that we did, no matter how well we thought we could hide our mistakes and shortcuts. And he knew every chef in Paris. He could truly make or break someone's career. Staying in that kitchen for as long as we could handle it was a sign of toughness and superiority that we all prided ourselves on.

And now I had thrown it all away. I'd worked for him for almost three years, and I'd just committed career suicide.

So I turned and walked back. Robuchon was in my station, finishing my dish.

"No, no," he said, pushing me away. "I don't need you."

That may have been true, but in that instant, I realized that I needed him. I needed my job. I could have done without the tactics, but I needed the instruction. I wanted the challenge of his elaborate dishes and his impossible sauces; I wanted to work in a place where chefs were breaking old rules and breaking new ground.

"No, I'll do it," I said and put on my apron.

He didn't say no. In fact, he didn't say anything. He just stayed there with me for a few minutes to make sure I finished the fish properly and returned to the pass. I could feel his eyes on me for the rest of the morning.

He didn't speak to me for three weeks. But wondering

when he would use this transgression against me was punishment enough.

That January, I got an offer to cook in Puerto Rico. The salary was amazing. The perks were fantastic and I would be living in an island paradise. I made plans to leave Robuchon when the restaurant closed in June for the summer holiday. I gave my notice six months before. But by June, the offer—which had always seemed too good to be true—had fallen through.

Robuchon called me into his office. He was a chameleon, and when he wasn't in the kitchen, where he felt that his reputation was always on the line, he was approachable and warm.

"Eric, I heard you're not going to Puerto Rico," he said. "Why didn't you tell me?"

I shrugged. "The deal fell through."

"Do you have something else?" He seemed genuinely concerned.

"No."

"Where would you like to go?" he asked.

"Brazil," I answered, honestly.

He shut that idea down immediately. "No," he said. "I am not sending you on a tropical vacation." I mentioned Spain, and he shook his head. "You live right next to Spain. Why don't you go somewhere new, somewhere farther away? We're closed in July, so take a few weeks off, get your head straight, and when you come back, I'll help you find a job."

Somehow, I made it unscathed until almost the end. And then, leading into the final lunch service before the restaurant closed for vacation and I left for Moissac, I prepared a sauce that I knew wasn't good enough. It was a really difficult recipe for a dish that had just been put on the menu: John Dory topped with delicate fried rings of fresh onion and served with a refined sauce based on onion jus. It wasn't his best dish, but I was still responsible for it. I had foolishly decided not to chop all of the onions I needed for the reduction—and I could taste it in the weakness of the flavor. I began to panic, but there was no time to start again.

"Show me your sauce," said Robuchon, suddenly behind me. I handed him a spoonful, meeting his gaze as he tasted it.

His eyes sparkled as he said with a friendly smile, "See, Ripert? I told you so." Meaning: you'll never be a saucier.

Then, he softened. "It's okay. You can send it."

I went home to Andorra for vacation, with a fun side trip to Spain. Shortly before I was to return to Paris, I got a call from Robuchon. True to his word, he had found me a job.

"So. I received a call from a good friend in Washington, Jean-Louis Palladin." I knew about Palladin: he was, they said, playful and passionate, energetic and fearless, a great French chef who had a very American verve. He had landed in Washington, D.C., opening a place at the Watergate Hotel and becoming a kind of rock star in the States. "He needs a chef de partie with the potential of becoming sous-chef, and I recommended you."

"America? I don't think I'm ready. And besides, I don't speak English."

He smiled—kindly, I thought. "You have proven yourself to be a fast learner. And you have certain skills. So it's decided?"

"I would be honored, Chef."

. . .

Leaving Robuchon was unexpectedly bittersweet. I knew from the moment I finished my last shift at Jamin that I was leaving my mentor behind. He taught me discipline. He taught me technique. He taught me skills. He taught me flavor. He taught me speed. He taught me how to be a cook. Maybe I'm biased or even brainwashed, but I believe that Joël Robuchon is one of the defining chefs of not only my generation, but of the twentieth century. In terms of excellence, there are no standouts who can compete with what he did and the influence he wielded.

The longer I was away from him, the more I could see that Robuchon had a quality of *wabi-sabi* about him: the beauty of imperfection. Just like the beautiful tea bowls that Japanese artisans purposefully nick or chip at the bottom as a quiet reminder that there is no such thing as perfection, so was Robuchon flawed with his frustration and his temper. His food was divine, but the chef was a man, with all of the nicks and chips that make us human.

24

:::

The Farm

Georges was retired and so was I, at least until my visa came through. I decided to spend the time waiting for my travel papers at the farm in Moissac, with short trips to Andorra and Spain. Supposedly I was there to spend time with Bernadette, but every morning at dawn I'd slip out of her bed and walk the dirt road to Georges's house. After drinking a terrible cup of coffee—the ninety-year-old house-keeper brewed it in the fireplace, using an old sock for a filter—we'd drive to the market in Moissac in his beautiful Mercedes. In those days, you still bought your ingredients for the day, not the week, which meant that we always had the perfect excuse to get out.

No matter how shabby his sweater or how thick he liked to lay on his rural accent, Georges was the king of the market. Everyone in town knew exactly how much land he owned and what his farm had yielded the year before. He was stopped at every stall to chat with old friends or answer questions about this year's crops. His route always began at the covered vegetable market in the town square, buying whatever he didn't grow and pointing out produce that he could tell had been trucked in from other regions.

As soon as Georges entered the market, the vendors pulled their best items out of crates that they kept under their tables. He was truly committed to quality. He'd spend thirty minutes talking to the woman selling beans about how she grew the *haricots Tarbais* and how she liked to make cassoulet, taking a deep interest in her methods—or so it seemed. The knowing looks that women gave him as we passed from stall to stall and on to the café made me think of stories I still heard from my cousins and uncles about my father—what a ladies' man he had been. I was too young to remember my father as a flirt, but I took a kind of familial pride in watching Georges in action.

After the café, we'd make our way to the bakery, the butcher, the cheesemonger, and occasionally the fishmonger. I never set foot in the fishmonger's, due to an incident with a man selling oysters while I was in the army: when I'd gotten back to the farm and opened them for our lunch, they were no longer moving. I immediately asked Georges to drive me back to town, where I quietly told the vendor that the oysters were dead and asked for my money back. I thought I was doing him a favor by letting him know he had a bad batch. But he refused to take them.

"You don't know anything about oysters," he said, waving me away as he would any skinny twentysomething.

I looked to Georges to make sure it was okay to argue with the guy.

"Sir, believe me: I do. I have worked with beautiful oysters in the restaurants where I've cooked. And I have never opened a dead one until today."

"He cooked for Joël Robuchon!" Georges interjected, trying to be helpful.

"Ah, a Parisian. Well then, you really don't know anything," the man said. At that point, I got so angry that I upended the sack of oysters and dumped them on the floor before storming out of the building.

I called the sanitation services from the phone in the café, where Georges had ordered us wine to celebrate.

"You were right, Eric," said Georges as he clinked my glass. "You should always stand up for quality." I was glad to know I had Georges's support, but the whole ordeal ruined the fishmonger's for me.

My favorite part of going to town with Georges was our visit to the foie gras market. In Gascony, foie gras was something that you prepared at home during the winter and ate for Sunday suppers and special occasions. At least a hundred farmers carefully displayed their ducks and geese, arranging them on white tablecloths as though they were presenting rings at Cartier. And they were definitely valuable—at least, their livers were. The foie gras market is where Georges truly became a legend in my eyes.

"*Le foie est petit,*" he'd say after barely caressing a freshly plucked mallard or goose. "*Le foie est gros,*" he'd murmur, lightly running his hand along another. I still don't know how he did it. He didn't press them or prod them or even pick them up. He just brushed his fingers against their cool, nubby carcasses to feel how plump the liver was. Sometimes he could tell simply by looking. Bluish-black skin meant that the animal had been brutalized and the liver would be damaged too. And he was never wrong. He bought only the most impeccable foie.

We never made it home before eleven in the morning. The *doméstique* would unload the car as we set about making lunch in the fireplace. Georges's wife, Guillemette, would sometimes braise a hare in one corner of the fireplace. She'd cook it for two whole days and when she was done, it fell right off the bone. The pleasure of the smell, the pleasure of lifting the lid and seeing the evolution of the dish—to cook that dish gave you the illusion that you had all the time in the world. It was very different from restaurant cooking, where you were always working against time to make each dish perfect—and fast as you could. That hare could've cooked for two days, or five. There was no rush on Georges's farm.

The ceiling of the house was hung with hams and *saucisson,* which collected the smoke. When it was summertime and the small house smoldered with heat, the preserved meats would be moved into the cellar dug below the house. This was where the confit was kept.

In the kitchen, Georges also liked to prepare *chou farci* and braised pork neck with green olives, adding a little bit of flour to thicken the rich sauce. I cooked whenever I could, sometimes adapting Robuchon dishes for fun. If we were making *moules marinières,* I would take the mussels out of their shells and arrange them on each plate in the shape of a snail, dressing them with a sauce made from mayonnaise, crème fraîche, mussel juice, and lemon juice. But mostly I kept it simple. Although the last four years had taught me craftsmanship and instilled an appreciation for quality at the highest level, it was a relief to be able to improvise, to pay attention to the true nature of the ingredients.

Georges and his family often grilled carcasses of ducks and geese in the fireplace and made the most incredible French fries cooked in duck fat. And yet, as far as I can tell, even all these years later, no one ever had a problem with cholesterol. Everyone lived to be eighty.

Just as Georges selected his birds, so did I trust my hands to tell me about the produce—to tell, from touch, if a tomato might be watery and flavorless, or thick-skinned and starchy, and then pick a better one. And then I let my instinct tell me how to prepare it, without putting all of my effort into the presentation. For once, I knew what it felt like to cook with my heart and soul, just like my grandmother in Nice. Even if I was only roasting a chicken or making a pizza *à la française*, this country cooking was as liberating as it was satisfying. I was making what I wanted for the first time in my life, and I was doing it for people I cared about. To be able to watch someone's face as they tasted my food was a new thrill, and something that never got old.

"You know, Eric," Bernadette's mom said one day as we ate lunch under the chestnut tree, "I heard there's a job opening in the hospital cafeteria. All you'd have to do is open cans! Imagine how much easier that would be than going to America."

I smiled, not wanting to look down on hospital cooks, but I was confident that no matter what Robuchon claimed my failings were, that kind of job would not be my fate.

In the afternoons, Georges and I would walk the fields to see what was ready to be harvested. He explained how each fruit and vegetable was cultivated to his specifications, starting with their planting during the appropriate moon. During my visits between Andorra and the ocean that summer, I watched apricots ripen to the color of sunsets, cherries get fat and sweet, artichoke plants grow tall and spiked with purple thistles. In early September, when I moved into Bernadette's fulltime, the special golden Chasselas grapes were ready. Then there were the apples, red and juicy, like candy hanging from a tree, followed by the pears. Georges strolled us through the cool, corrugated-steel warehouse to make sure that produce was being properly sorted, boxed, and stored for export. After that we would stop by the animal pens out back to count the eggs and pet the pigs. When I was a kid, I gathered eggs and picked up fresh milk on the small farms where my mother and I had lived, but this was a real operation. I was in heaven.

Obviously I wasn't a farmer—these were people who could predict the weather based on which way the wind was blowing. But I tried helping out a few times, even though it wasn't expected of me. (Like Georges, I enjoyed a special retiree status.) In July I spent a single morning destroying my hands in an attempt to harvest artichokes, and an hour or two running apples through the sorter in the fall. I was invited to kill chickens, but politely said I'd rather see how they did it first. The chickens were stupid: you could just pick them up and slit their throats before they knew what had happened. But the pigs were smart. Worse (for me), the family treated them as pets, naming them and petting them right up until the minute they called them into the pen to be killed in the winter.

The first one trotted in when he heard them call *"Viens viens viens!"* Georges briskly slit the pig's throat while a few workers held him. The animal's cries were chillingly human. I was even more traumatized by the sight of blood everywhere—it reminded me of Hugo in my mother's bathroom. The second pig frantically looked for his friend when he heard his name called. Once he realized what had happened, he refused to go into the pen. I went back into the house, unable to watch. Later, I had a hard time helping them break down the bled-out animal for the winter's hams, sausages, and *boudin noir*. I knew that they respected the animals' lives, but I wasn't able to help them close the cycle.

However, I was allowed to attend one sacred ritual that the other men on the farm were not: the making of the foie gras. The men weren't even allowed into the house during the days it was being prepared, since it was feared that their dirt-caked hands and shoes would contaminate the jars and cans of confited liver that would make their meals so satisfying and be pulled out on special occasions throughout the year.

"We've never allowed a single man in here," Georges's wife said to me with a wink. "You, you're the exception." The other women giggled and put their heads back down to the serious task at hand.

For two days each week after the holidays, the women in the community turned the big farm kitchen into a preservation laboratory. The Mercedes-loads of geese and mallards that Georges brought home were methodically broken down and separated into their useful parts. First the duck legs and breasts were layered with salt and bay leaves and left overnight to cure. The next day, the salt was washed off and the meat slowly cooked in the fat that had been rendered in massive copper pots, filling the house with a strong aroma, like rasher after rasher of bacon being fried on a Sunday morning. At dinner, we grilled the carcasses in the fireplace and shared the charred bits of meat, licking our fingers with relish.

The corn-fattened livers were carefully deveined and soaked in milk to draw out any bitterness before being canned. In Gascony, it was sacrilegious to eat foie gras medium-rare, or *mi-cuit:* it had to be well done. The brownish-yellow lobes were sliced and put into cans, then boiled in a giant kettle, where they cooked in their own fat. Throughout the process, everything was exactingly sterilized and measured—a single crumb or missing gram of salt could spoil a valuable batch. After each jar and can had been boiled, we carefully labeled them and arranged them in the cellar. The day the pigs were slaughtered, we set about confiting and canning the pork loin, which would be sliced like ham come summer. We marked the end of our month of labor with a big celebration dinner.

I didn't realize it at the time, but my months at the farm, working with meat—the pigs and the ducks and the geese—added a muscularity to my cooking that would hold me in good stead when I got to America and the next stage of my career. Fish, which is what I did for Robuchon, is more technical, but meat is more sensual. At the time, I was more of an intellectual chef. But it's important to have both—the instinct and the technique, the elegance and the muscular sensuality—to be a great chef.

For those weeks, I felt like I was back at my grandparents' in Nîmes for the making of the *conserves au tomate.* My grandfather and I would harvest as many tomatoes as we could, pulling them home in a cart. My grandmother blanched, peeled, and seeded them, packing them into clean jars, while my grandfather fed wood into the stove in the backyard. The jars went into the big pressurized washtub that was used to boil the linen sheets. I spent hours going from the kitchen to the stove, inhaling the sweet smoke in the thick August air. The next day, we'd move on to string beans. In Andorra in the fall, I also helped my mother put up the wild mushrooms that we harvested in our special spots in the mountains around our home. The pop of a jar unsealing in winter still makes me nostalgic.

Every two or three weeks, I drove the four hours back to Andorra to see my mother, climb mountains, and get away from Bernadette. Things were better with her only in that I spent most of my time with Georges. She was back at her job in the gift shop in town for most of the day. When we were home in Moissac, our fights weren't as bad because her family was there. (Jean-Claude was always studying, so I said we had to respect his silence.) Also, I had adapted to the farmer's way of living: sleep when the sun goes down, wake when it rises. We didn't overlap that often, but when we did, it was a disaster. We were both so young, and I didn't know how to take the time to make her feel assured of my love, when all of my energy was poured into my career, any more than she knew how to manage her insecurities.

In Moissac, being so close to the source of the food and the rhythm of nature made me appreciate my job as a cook even more, and I was itching to get back to building my career. I didn't want to leave Georges, but the winter months had cut our market mornings and field walks short. (November through February were mostly about maintaining the trees.) As much as I loved the smell of the icy soil and hay mixing with cut branches and wood smoke, I wasn't used to being away from a restaurant kitchen for so long. I was eager to get back to work. The joke about the job at the hospital cafeteria was starting to get old. I started calling D.C. every two days, increasingly anxious to move on to the next phase of my life.

Still, even now, whenever I cook a rustic lunch over a fire I think about Georges and all he taught me about the beauty of a simple meal. I grew up in a small village, but Andorra was a little more cosmopolitan. Before Georges, I had never had any contact with a real gentleman farmer. I had no real experience with rural living. Georges and the people who worked for him were amazingly efficient in every way. They used every bit of land they owned, they used every part of the food they got.

Georges and his extended group of family and friends were—and remain—great, great people. They prepared me for my next stage of cooking—working for Jean-Louis Palladin. Palladin was from that part of the country and that's what his cooking was about: the powerful flavors of meats and innards, the transformative power of fat saved from meat and fowl. I'd just come from Jamin, one of the most refined kitchens in the world. Although I didn't know it yet, if I hadn't had those months on the farm, I would have never understood Jean-Louis.

Every time I cook on a fireplace, it all comes rushing back: the hams hanging, the grandma stewing the hare, fries in duck fat, the morning coffee cooked on an open flame. Georges's greatest gift is how this all lives on in me. It was a very happy time in my life, and that was an important lesson too: to learn how little it took to be happy, to understand from a young age that the human heart is a small and delicate vase. You must handle it carefully, but in the right circumstances, it does not take much to fill it up.

Finally, that March, Jean-Louis Palladin's cool, raspy voice came on the line and told me that the visa had come through at last. He wanted me there in April.

I knew that I had to break up with Bernadette for the last time. If we didn't, it would just keep dragging on. She'd come to Andorra. She'd probably find me in Washington.

"Here's what I'll do," I told her as she sat on the edge of her bed. "You know that the relationship that we have is very bad."

She started to protest, but I kept talking. "I'm going there with no money, and neither of us speaks English. If it's bad, it'll be like Paris but worse. We should end it."

She began to cry. "It's not that I don't want to be a normal person," she said. "I don't want to make a scandal every time we're together. It's just . . . I can't control you, and I can't control myself. You're right: you should go."

Saying goodbye to Georges was harder. I knew that we would remain friends, but I also knew that America was far away and he was already an old man. Thinking of my father's death, I wondered if I should attempt to say goodbye just in case I never saw him again. Early the next morning, the coffee brewing in the fireplace, I tried to start, but he waved away all my attempts at sentimentalism.

"You think because I'm just a simple farmer that you'll be

done with me?" he joked. "Just because you're going to cook for the president of the United States in Washington, D.C., doesn't mean I won't have a thing or two to teach you when you come home."

I began to explain that I wasn't going to cook for the president. I was going to Washington, D.C., not the White House. But Georges just laughed.

"I'm just having my fun," he said. Then he asked, "You taking Bernadette with you?"

"No, we're ending it."

"Don't feel guilty," Georges said. "She'll find herself another stray dog. Maybe the next one will like being kept on a leash." Then he laughed again, the kind of full-bodied laugh that filled the entire room. And it occurred to me that for the first time, in a long time, I was happy.

Georges, Raymond, Jacques, Maurice. In the year of changes ahead of me, I would often think of all of the good, wise men who touched my life. Could it be that, somehow, my father sent them? Pointed them toward me, as guides, to help complete the work he could not? My father died when I was young. That is the central tragedy of my life. But his spirit never left me, and that may be the defining miracle of my life.

25

:::

A Decision

I packed only one suitcase for my move to America, with some sweaters and my knives. The restaurant would provide my uniform, and I could buy whatever clothes I needed once I got there with the money my mother had given me. Besides, who knew what would come of this job. I remember thinking, *I might be back in a month.* I had no idea that I was about to build an entire life in America, that I would never again live in France. One suitcase, and it wasn't even packed to the gills. Perhaps unconsciously, I was leaving room for all of the possibilities.

To get to America, I would have to take two planes—one from Toulouse to Paris and another from Paris to Washington,

D.C. My mother drove me to the airport in Toulouse and, as we had so many times before, we drove to the top of the mountain and there at the very top, we crossed the border from Andorra to France. When we got to the border, my mother stopped the car and gave the customs agents our documents. I remember her saying, with great pride, "My son has been invited to be a chef in America. Look at him, he's still just a kid and he's already made his name in Paris. They have invited him abroad."

Usually I would try to shush her, have her not embarrass me. During that last visit, I took great pains to point out that I was twenty-four years old. "Hey, I'm not a kid, I'm a man." But my mother insisted on billing me as a child prodigy. While she bragged about me to the customs agents, I sat quietly, lost in my own thoughts. I was deeply aware that I was turning a page, that I was—in my young life—at the top of the mountain in more ways than one. My childhood was over. I knew that I would never live in Andorra again, that I would never again have this back and forth of living with Mom. I had this sixth sense telling me, "This is over. You're going to America and you will never come back to Andorra in the same way."

I was not yet a Buddhist, but I had this very Zen moment of being absolutely and completely in the present. We couldn't have spent more than thirty minutes at the border and yet time slowed down so much that it felt like days. I looked at the mountains where I had hiked and cooked with my family and friends. This was the backdrop to the happiest moments I can remember and even that was a kind of revelation: my life had seemed so hard, but it felt good to look out at the bright blue sky and be able to recall so much happiness. I remember feeling a certain nostalgia because as much as I wanted to, I couldn't take the mountains with me. Once we cleared border control and my mother's car began its downhill descent, there were even more goodbyes. We were in France, but France for me was done. Whatever I had done in Paris, that was over too. I knew I would never go back to the world of Robuchon and Jamin. Twice was enough.

Years after my father passed away, my sister ran into some of the friends who had been with him on the mountaintop when he died. Apparently, he was holding his camera and peering through the lens right before he collapsed. "You go ahead," he had encouraged them. "I want to take some pictures." But his friends were in no rush, so they were just a few feet away when he began to snap photo after photo. Cameras were big mechanical boxes back in the late 1970s and one friend in particular remembered the sound of my father taking pictures, the click of each image being captured on film. All of the friends remembered his last words and it was a story they had discussed many times over the years. Before he passed away, before he dropped the camera and his heart stopped, my father looked through the lens and said, "Oh, it's so beautiful." I often wondered what exactly he saw through the camera as he gazed at the end of his life. I thought of him as we drove to the airport because I knew that, in my own way, I was seeing things for the first and the last time.

In Paris, everyone I cooked with—with rare exceptions— was French. There is a shorthand, a sameness that you come to take for granted, under those circumstances. I had very little fear about my new life because I thought anything would be easier than Robuchon. I did not realize how extremely naïve I was about America. First of all, I didn't speak English. I thought, *Jean Louis is going to be kind to me because he's French. We're going to speak in French. He's going to be cool.*

Then my ego started kicking in: *You know they probably need me in America because I'm a great cook. I came from Robuchon and now I'm going to come to America.* I thought there'd be a kind of culinary red carpet for me at the airport. I had no idea of the struggle ahead of me and how it would humble me. I did not know it yet, but an American restaurant kitchen is the perfect place for an immigrant to find his way: I would be surrounded by people who did not speak English as their first language, who know deeply and profoundly what it feels like to leave your country, without a safety net, to leave everything and everyone you know behind.

I also did not think that I would spend decades in America. I thought I was going for a training stint: three years, tops. My dream was to open a restaurant in Spain, my own mash-up of Jacques's place in Andorra and the kind of innovative cooking we were doing at Jamin: a small, intimate restaurant, with great service and great cuisine. I had vacationed in Spain since I was a teenager, and it had always been a fun place. I imagined I would end up there: pursuing a Michelin star or two, but also making sure that I had a great quality of life.

I knew that America would be an important part of my development as a chef, but I did not think, at twenty-four, that it would become home. Once I said goodbye to my mother, once I de-boarded the short flight from Toulouse to Paris, I set my mind on the adventure ahead of me.

Who would I be in America? Nobody knew me there, so I had—I thought—the opportunity to choose. I would be authoritative and modern like Bouchet, strong in technique and spirit like Maurice, creative and maybe a little unpredictable like Robuchon, dedicated and joyful like Georges.

I sometimes wondered why I hadn't gone into banking like

my father or become an entrepreneur like my mother. While it is true that I developed a taste for luxury early—I can still picture myself in Jacques's kitchen at age thirteen, the two of us eating spoonfuls of Beluga caviar, scooping it straight from the tin—I have always liked the practicality of kitchen life: the way that every meal begins not with fireworks but a foundation of well-honed basics, a well-executed mise en place, and an appreciation for the ingredients. Georges was never in the kitchen like Maurice and Jacques, but he could see it in me: the dedication to the basics, the desire to master each dish and technique, the way that cooking was a mountain that I would patiently and joyfully hike until I made it to the top.

For whatever reason, I wasn't nervous when my mother left me at the Toulouse airport, perhaps because this car ride was so different from the monumental ones we had taken before. I was not eight, being exiled to boarding school. I was not fifteen, a kid headed off to my second-choice culinary college. I was not even the seventeen-year-old arriving for work at La Tour d'Argent. My boyhood had wounded me but, in time, I had managed to gather the pieces together into something that felt fairly whole.

During my transfer at Charles de Gaulle, I had just a handful of francs left, so I went to the newsstand. I picked up an issue of *Playboy*, thinking it a very adult purchase. But on the way to the cash register, a book on a low shelf caught my eye: it was about Tibet. Much like the moment when I had to decide between a date and my first dinner at Jamin, I found myself deciding between an immediate pleasure and the opening of a door that could change my world. There was so much I wanted to get out of my trip to the States, and achievement in my field and romantic love were high on my list. The book about Tibet seemed to offer something that I did not realize I was missing: it spoke to the possibility for peace—not in the global sense but a peace that could exist in one's life and in one's heart. When the announcer said that my flight was boarding, I acted on instinct. I dropped the *Playboy,* grabbed the book, and ran to my gate.

Back then the airport had an elaborate system of calling passengers from one waiting room to the next until you finally boarded a bus that carried you out onto the tarmac, where you climbed—in the fresh air—a giant set of stairs up to the plane. I had a lot of time to think, and as I would do so often in the months and years to come, I thought of Robuchon.

He had shattered my confidence and instilled a kind of fear in me that even now defies explanation. As terrified as I was of Robuchon, I stayed at Jamin, and returned for a second tour, because I knew that he was teaching me more than I could have learned anywhere else. Though this was hard to keep in mind while he was yelling at me for my mistakes and while I cursed at him under my breath, he wasn't just breaking me for the sake of breaking me. He was molding me, and the other young chefs he had chosen to be part of Jamin, in his image.

In Robuchon's kitchen every ingredient was precious; nothing was to be taken for granted. For him, everything that we touched, from the smallest fava bean to a sliver of black truffle to a tablespoon of caviar, was equally alive and therefore important. Robuchon taught me that no ingredient is humble; every ingredient is sacred. It has been many years now and I have been shaped by many other chefs, but there are moments—like when I grab a tray of tomatoes—when I hear his voice urging me to respect the fact that even a tomato is precious, and it is as if I'm twenty again and he is walking beside me. In those moments what I remember is not the pain, but the possibility. It's like the Buddhist author Shunryu Suzuki wrote: "In the beginner's mind, there are many possibilities. In the expert's mind, there are few." I had spent the better part of three years challenged by Robuchon's requests. But because of him, I was headed to America, a place I had dreamed of living since I was a boy. I knew then that he had seen something in me—not just a lack of skill, because the skills would come—but in all of my blankness, an endless span of possibility.

Acknowledgments

My mother, Monique, is a remarkable woman. It was at her table that I first learned my love of food. She saw my passion for cooking; she encouraged and supported me; and it was through her that this whole world was opened.

My father was only in my life for a short time, but he inspired me with his passion, his curiosity, and his *joie de vivre*. He loved me a lot and I *felt* his love. I still do.

My beloved wife, Sandra, fills my life with love and laughter. I work very hard and I'm very focused, but she makes this journey a joyful one.

One day, my son, Adrien, will read this book. I want him to know how proud I am to be his father and what an inspiration it is to have him as my son.

My grandmothers, Maguy and Emilienne, were two of my earliest teachers in the kitchen. The food they prepared, and the love they poured into each meal, showed me the importance of cooking with both my head and heart.

Sandra, Adrien, and I are fortunate to be surrounded by a large and loving extended family. This book was written with great affection and appreciation for you all.

Veronica Chambers, my writing partner, spent hundreds of hours in the basement of Le Bernardin, listening to my story and transforming our conversations into words on the page. She does not speak French. She is not a trained cook. And yet somehow she captured my life in full, bringing to life the people and the places that shaped who I am as a man and a chef. I am grateful for my dear Veronica, her work and her friendship. There would be no book without her.

Cathy Sheary, director of strategic partnerships at Le Bernardin, was an essential partner in the book process. She cleared the decks for me to dive into this book, managed all the teams involved, and was a thoughtful, patient participant in the creative process from beginning to end.

Susan Kamil, Susan Mercandetti, and Kim Witherspoon believed I had a memoir in me, long before I was convinced of the fact. I'm grateful to the team at Random House, especially Andy Ward and Kaela Myers. Thanks are due, as well, to the talented Becca Parrish and her team at Becca PR.

This book first began to take shape when I traveled to France and Andorra with my friend Christine Muhlke. Our conversations and her thoughts helped me lay the foundation for the work you hold in your hands. *Merci,* Christine.

Above all, this book is a tribute to my mentors and to the generosity of spirit that is at the heart of my industry. We do not learn how to cook from books. This is a field in which knowledge is passed as we stand, side by side, in tight quarters where the stoves are hot and the knives are sharp. I am thankful for the mentorship of a stellar array of chefs: Jacques Quillacq, Gilbert Le Coze, Jean-Louis Palladin, Dominique Bouchet, and the inimitable Joël Robuchon. I'm also thankful for two cherished friends: my old friend from culinary school days, Raymond Centène, and a great gentleman farmer from Gascony, Georges Desbouges.

I am forever grateful to my dear friend and business partner, Maguy Le Coze, and the extraordinary team at Le Bernardin, including Chris Muller, Ben Chekroun, Aldo Sohm, and many others. Maurice Guillouet and Eric "Coco" Gestel cooked with me when I was in my early twenties, deep in the weeds, at Jamin. When does the second team come in, Coco? The answer is never!

ERIC RIPERT is the chef and co-owner of the New York restaurant Le Bernardin, which holds three stars in the Michelin Guide and has maintained a four-star review from *The New York Times* for more than three decades. He is vice chairman of the board of City Harvest, a New York–based food rescue organization, as well as a recipient of the Legion d'Honneur, France's highest honor. He is the host of his own TV series, *Avec Eric,* which has won Emmy and James Beard awards. Ripert is the author of five cookbooks: *Avec Eric, On the Line, A Return to Cooking, Le Bernardin Cookbook: Four Star Simplicity,* and *My Best: Eric Ripert.*

le-bernardin.com

Facebook.com/ChefEricRipert

@ericripert